GEORGIA TRIVIA

GEORGIA TRIVIA

Compiled by
ERNIE & JILL COUCH

REVISED EDITION

Rutledge Hill Press®
Nashville, Tennessee
A Thomas Nelson Company

Published by Rutledge Hill Press, a Thomas Nelson Company,
P.O. Box 141000, Nashville, Tennessee 37214.

Typography by D&T/Bailey Typesetting, Inc.

Library of Congress Cataloging-in-Publication Data

Couch, Ernie, 1949–
  Georgia trivia.

  1. Georgia—Miscellanea. 2. Questions and answers.
  I. Couch, Jill, 1948–   . II. Title.
F286.5.C68 1986 975.8
ISBN 1-55853-228-5

Printed in the United States of America
4 5 6 7 8 9 — 05 04 03 02 01 00

PREFACE

As the paramount of both Classic and New South, Georgia stands as a blend of age old traditions, steeped in hospitality, and the latest in high-tech advancement. Georgia's colorful and compelling history speaks of a richly diversified land and people. Captured within these pages are some of the highlights of this rich heritage, both the known and the not so well known.

Georgia Trivia is designed to be informative, educational and entertaining. But most of all we hope that you will be motivated to learn more about the great state of Georgia.

Ernie & Jill Couch

To
Mary Bray Wheeler,
Berry Henderson Couch
and
the great people of Georgia

TABLE OF CONTENTS

GEOGRAPHY

C H A P T E R   O N E

Q. How many counties are there in Georgia?

A. 159.

———◆———

Q. The annual Miss Georgia pageant is hosted by what city?

A. Columbus.

———◆———

Q. Which county is the newest in the state?

A. Peach, created July 18, 1924.

———◆———

Q. In which time zone is Georgia situated?

A. Eastern.

———◆———

Q. Completed in 1992, Atlanta's C&S Plaza is how tall?

A. 1,050 feet, 57 stories.

Q. What community is the Apple Capital of Georgia?

A. Ellijay.

———◆———

Q. Which states border Georgia?

A. Florida, Alabama, Tennessee, North Carolina, and South Carolina.

———◆———

Q. What does the town name *Dahlonega* mean in the Cherokee language?

A. "Precious yellow metal" (gold).

———◆———

Q. Where was the novel *Gone with the Wind* written?

A. In Atlanta, on Crescent Avenue.

———◆———

Q. Where is the Peach Blossom Trail situated?

A. On US 341 north of Perry.

———◆———

Q. In the 1890s what was the communal-type society established in Ware County called?

A. Ruskin.

———◆———

Q. What museum, featuring more than thirty historical airplanes, is in Warner Robins?

A. Robins Air Force Base Museum of Aviation.

Q. The South's largest Civil War–period sword factory was in what city?

A. Columbus.

———◆———

Q. What is the name of the lower region of Charlton County, which is bordered on three sides by the state of Florida?

A. Big Bend.

———◆———

Q. What is former President Jimmy Carter's hometown?

A. Plains.

———◆———

Q. What neighborhood has the distinction of being Atlanta's first suburb?

A. Inman Park, circa 1890.

———◆———

Q. The world's second bottler of Coca-Cola, E. R. Barber, was from what Georgia city?

A. Valdosta.

———◆———

Q. What is the total land and inland water area of the state?

A. 58,910 square miles.

———◆———

Q. What river forms much of the northeastern boundary of the state?

A. Savannah.

Q. How long is the Georgia section of the Appalachian Trail?

A. Seventy-eight miles.

Q. What is the oldest recorded placename in Georgia?

A. The Apalachee River, noted by the Spanish in 1528.

Q. What is the name of the farm complex southeast of Juliette that was run from the 1840s to the 1940s and is now open to the public?

A. Jarrell Plantation.

Q. Where was Confederate hero William Thomas Overby born?

A. About ten miles east of Newnan.

Q. Helen is recognized for what type of architecture?

A. Bavarian Alpine.

Q. What name was given in 1926 to the 280-acre juvenile detention house development situated in Bibb County?

A. Smithsonia.

Q. Why has Georgia been called the Empire State of the South?

A. Because of its large size and thriving industries.

Q. The Blood Mountain Archeological Area in Union County was the site of a great battle between what two Indian tribes prior to the arrival of European explorers?

A. Cherokee and Creek.

———◆———

Q. Under the Confederacy, what city served as the temporary state capital from November 18, 1864, to March 11, 1865?

A. Macon.

———◆———

Q. Fort McPherson honors what Union officer?

A. James Birdseye McPherson, killed during the Atlanta Campaign of 1864.

———◆———

Q. Where did Mercer Institute, which later became Mercer University, open in 1833?

A. Penfield.

———◆———

Q. What is the greatest distance north to south in the state?

A. 315 miles.

———◆———

Q. What river forms the border between the southeastern corner of Georgia and the northeastern corner of Florida?

A. St. Marys.

———◆———

Q. What town is known as the City of Thirteen Highways?

A. Hawkinsville.

Q. What is the name of the South's largest department store?

A. Rich's Department Store, in Atlanta.

———◆———

Q. Which county borders both Alabama and Florida?

A. Seminole.

———◆———

Q. In what town is the antebellum home of Alexander H. Stephens, vice president of the Confederacy?

A. Crawfordville.

———◆———

Q. Approximately what percentage of Georgia's population is urban?

A. 60 percent.

———◆———

Q. From which two counties was a total of 255 square miles taken to form Ben Hill County on July 31, 1906?

A. Irwin and Wilcox.

———◆———

Q. Covering 28,000 acres, what is the largest college campus in the world?

A. Berry College.

———◆———

Q. What Monroe County community, established in 1966, is named for the type of cotton fabric produced by the Bibb Manufacturing Company for the manufacturing of sheets and pillowcases?

A. Percale.

Q. In 1861 the legislature of Georgia changed the name of which county to Bartow, to honor Confederate hero Colonel Francis S. Bartow?

A. Cass.

Q. What is the nickname of Athens?

A. Classic City.

Q. For whom is 2,990-foot-high Charlie Mountain in Rabun County named?

A. Charlie Hicks, a principal Cherokee chief.

Q. In what city are the national headquarters of the Centers for Disease Control?

A. Atlanta.

Q. What county was formed in 1856 by taking acreage from Coffee, Irwin, and Lowndes counties?

A. Berrien.

Q. What state park in Bartow County was developed in the 1930s for African Americans?

A. George Washington Carver State Park.

Q. An 1883 steam pumper for fire fighting, one of the oldest in the world, may be seen in what community?

A. Hawkinsville.

Q. Where can one see the Rock Eagle, a mound topped by the effigy of an outstretched bird with a 120-foot wingspread made of milky quartz stones, approximately 6,000 years old?

A. Eatonton.

———◆———

Q. What log structure situated on the north edge of Riverdale was designated Federal headquarters in August 1864, from which Generals Sherman and Thomas transmitted and received dispatches?

A. The Drew Couch house.

———◆———

Q. What community in Dougherty County was given its name because it is in the center of the world's leading papershell pecan region?

A. Pecan City.

———◆———

Q. What was the first British fort built in Georgia?

A. Fort King George, on the Altamaha River, in 1721.

———◆———

Q. What is Georgia's southernmost coastal island?

A. Cumberland.

———◆———

Q. What town, situated 1,395 feet above sea level, has the name of the Italian word meaning "high"?

A. Alto.

———◆———

Q. Upon its completion in 1927, the Juliette Grist Mill held what world record?

A. World's largest water-powered gristmill.

Q. Because of the moderate climate, by what nickname is the southeastern region of the United States, which includes Georgia, known?

A. The Sun Belt.

———◆———

Q. What town is situated at the junction of Bleckley, Laurens, Twiggs, and Wilkinson counties?

A. Allentown.

———◆———

Q. For whom was Jekyll Island named?

A. Sir Joseph Jekyll, the largest contributor to Georgia's colonization.

———◆———

Q. What community, situated in Wheeler County, is named for the famous San Antonio, Texas, mission meaning "cottonwood" or "poplar" in Spanish?

A. Alamo.

———◆———

Q. Where is the world's largest aircraft plant under one roof located?

A. Marietta, Lockheed Aircraft.

———◆———

Q. For what is Modoc in Emmanuel County named?

A. A northwestern Indian tribe.

———◆———

Q. The unique culture of coastal and sea-island blacks, known in South Carolina as Gullah, is called by what name in Georgia?

A. Geechee.

Q. What town states that it is the Garden Spot of the World and Southwest Georgia?

A. Arlington.

------◆------

Q. Where was the last official business of the treasury of the Confederate States transacted?

A. Sandersville.

------◆------

Q. What city is the capital of Georgia?

A. Atlanta.

------◆------

Q. What has been the location of the Georgia School for the Deaf since its first five students were admitted in 1846?

A. Cave Springs.

------◆------

Q. The 132-foot-long Cromer's Mill covered bridge of town lattice design, built in 1906, is in which county?

A. Franklin.

------◆------

Q. By what name was the coastal plain of Georgia known to the Spanish?

A. Gaule, pronounced "Wally."

------◆------

Q. The Georgia state legislature consists of how many representatives?

A. 180.

Q. What plantation was the largest and most famous of the St. Simons antebellum plantations?

A. Hamilton.

———◆———

Q. By what name is the convergence of several major thoroughfares that form Atlanta's hub known?

A. Five Points.

———◆———

Q. The city of Waycross is in what county?

A. Ware.

———◆———

Q. What Clay County town is known as the Queen City of the Chattahoochee?

A. Fort Gaines.

———◆———

Q. For whom was the town of Mitchell named?

A. R. M. Mitchell, president of the Augusta Southern Railroad.

———◆———

Q. What is the Candy Capital of Georgia?

A. Eastman.

———◆———

Q. What county was first organized as the Parish of St. George?

A. Burke.

Q. Where was a branch of the United States mint operated for twenty-three years for the purpose of striking gold coins?

A. Dahlonega.

Q. Where was the Georgia Baptist Convention organized on June 27, 1822?

A. Powelton.

Q. For whom was Fort Frederica on St. Simons Island named?

A. Frederick Louis, the British Prince of Wales.

Q. A Confederate gun shop originally was moved to what two Georgia towns during the Civil War?

A. Rome and Dawson.

Q. What town is known as the Broiler City?

A. Canton.

Q. What college is situated at Statesboro?

A. Georgia Southern.

Q. Black Rock Mountain State Park is situated in what town in Rabun County?

A. Mountain City.

Q. What is the nickname of Albany?

A. City of Opportunity.

———◆———

Q. The misreading of a post office application in Washington, D.C., for the Georgia community of Fox Valley in 1825 brought about what automatic name change?

A. A change to the name Fort Valley.

———◆———

Q. Where in Atlanta is the Cyclorama?

A. Grant Park.

———◆———

Q. What was the name of the post office established June 9, 1835, on the site of present-day Atlanta?

A. White Hall.

———◆———

Q. What body of water borders Clay, Quitman, and Stewart counties on the west?

A. The Walter F. George Reservoir or Lake George.

———◆———

Q. The whimsically named community of Hopeulikit is situated in what county?

A. Bulloch.

———◆———

Q. What is the location of Georgia Southwestern College?

A. Americus.

Q. The army's Fort Stewart is situated in which county?

A. Liberty.

———◆———

Q. What are the state colors?

A. Red, white, and blue.

———◆———

Q. Captain William A. Fuller, the Western and Atlantic Railroad conductor who led the recapturing of the General, a locomotive stolen by Andrews's Raiders at Big Shanty, April 12, 1862, was born in what city?

A. Morrow.

———◆———

Q. What waterway threads its way through the state's coastal islands?

A. The Atlantic Intracoastal Waterway.

———◆———

Q. Arnold Blum, who helped the United States win the 1957 Walker Cup Crown, is a native of what community?

A. Macon.

———◆———

Q. What community in Carroll County carries the name of a state?

A. Kansas.

———◆———

Q. What four-year Bible college at Toccoa is designed for students from missionary families living all over the world?

A. Toccoa Falls Institute.

Q. Where is the oldest continually used courthouse in the state?

A. Fayette County Courthouse, built in 1825 in Fayetteville.

———◆———

Q. For whom was Clarksville named?

A. Governor John C. Clark, 1819–1823.

———◆———

Q. Approximately how long is the Georgia coastline?

A. 100 miles.

———◆———

Q. Where was the home of General Jordan Bush, who as the last Confederate veteran from Georgia died in 1952 at the age of 107?

A. Fitzgerald.

———◆———

Q. What community about ten miles north of Valdosta is named for the Indian word meaning "much water"?

A. Mineola.

———◆———

Q. What was the most expensive British fortification built in North America?

A. Fort Frederica, St. Simons Island.

———◆———

Q. Known as the Christmas Town of Georgia, what town features streets with Christmas-related names?

A. Bethlehem.

Q. Cairo is noted for being the center of what type of trade in the state?

A. The syrup trade.

———◆———

Q. What was the name of the first Scottish colony in Georgia, situated in McIntosh County?

A. New Inverness, later renamed Darien.

———◆———

Q. Near what present-day town was the Great Buffalo Lick found?

A. Philomath.

———◆———

Q. The majority of the Okefenokee Swamp is in which two counties?

A. Charlton and Ware.

———◆———

Q. Where was the largest and most effective private armory in the Confederacy situated?

A. Athens, Cook and Brother Armory.

———◆———

Q. Moultrie is on what river?

A. The Ocklockney.

———◆———

Q. Covering 284 square miles, what is the world's largest infantry camp?

A. Fort Benning, near Columbus.

Q. What is the name of the one-time plantation house, tavern, trading post, and post office found in Toccoa?

A. Traveler's Rest.

Q. In what Atlanta neighborhood is the Governor's Mansion?

A. Buckhead.

Q. Burke, Camden, Chatham, Effingham, Glynn, Liberty, Richmond, and Wilkes counties, formed in 1777, are known by what name?

A. Constitutional Counties.

Q. What is the highest elevation in the state?

A. 4,784 feet above sea level, Brasstown Bald Mountain.

Q. For whom was Effingham County named?

A. The English Lord Effingham, a supporter of colonial rights during the Revolutionary War.

Q. For whose estate in France was La Grange named?

A. Marquis de Lafayette.

Q. What is the largest religious group in the state?

A. Baptist.

Q. Where did Eli Whitney establish his first cotton gin?

A. Smyrna in Wilkes County.

———◆———

Q. The Lewis B. Wilson Airport in Macon was first known by what name?

A. Cochran Field.

———◆———

Q. What is the perimeter mileage of the state?

A. 1,051 miles.

———◆———

Q. In what city is the Doll Gallery, featuring more than 1,500 dolls?

A. Kennesaw.

———◆———

Q. The B. F. Goodrich Company established what town in Upham County in 1929 and annexed into Thomaston in 1958?

A. Silverton.

———◆———

Q. In 1971 the Modern States Life Insurance Company purchased what 3,200-foot-high mountain in Rabun County?

A. Screamer Mountain.

———◆———

Q. What community is known as the Crossroads of Georgia because it is very close to the geographic center of the state?

A. Perry.

Q. From what Georgia county were Treutlen, Laurens, Johnson, Telfair, Dodge, Jenkins, Emanuel, Bulloch, Tatnall, Toombs, and Wheeler counties taken?

A. Montgomery.

———◆———

Q. Ellen Louise Axson married Woodrow Wilson in 1885 in what Georgia city?

A. Savannah.

———◆———

Q. What community is known as the Carpet Capital of the World?

A. Dalton.

———◆———

Q. What is the county seat of Chattooga County?

A. Summerville.

———◆———

Q. The state of Georgia purchased Jekyll Island in what year?

A. 1947.

———◆———

Q. Henry B. Holliday, father of notorious western gunman John Henry ("Doc") Holliday, served as the first court clerk in which county?

A. Spalding.

———◆———

Q. Which community is noted for its world-famous, old-fashioned fruit cakes?

A. Claxton, Claxton Bakery, Inc.

Q. The county line between Johnson and Emanuel counties forms a large *Z* through which community?

A. Adrian.

Q. What was the only college for men that remained open during the Civil War?

A. Mercer University.

Q. Moody Air Force Base in Lowndes–Lanier counties is named after what man?

A. George Putnam Moody, a graduate of West Point.

Q. What city is known as Fountain City?

A. Columbus.

Q. Mule Camp Springs was the early name for what present-day community?

A. Gainesville.

Q. Erected in 1861, the last remaining Confederate flagpole is situated in what community?

A. Blakely.

Q. What state park, situated on the shore of Lake Blackshear in Crisp County, is named in honor of men and women from the state who served in World Wars I and II?

A. Georgia Veterans Memorial State Park.

Q. Blakely is known by what nickname?

A. Peanut Capital of the World.

———◆———

Q. To what did Berlin in Colquitt County change its name temporarily during World War I?

A. Lens.

———◆———

Q. When was the nickname Gate City first applied to Atlanta?

A. 1857, in a toast at a banquet given in Charleston, South Carolina.

———◆———

Q. What is the meaning of the term *piedmont,* which is applied to the region of the state between the Appalachians and the coastal plains?

A. "Foot hills."

———◆———

Q. What is the name of the restored 1836 stagecoach inn in Lumpkin?

A. Bedingfield Inn.

———◆———

Q. How many acres are included in the Chattahoochee National Forest?

A. 739,252 acres.

———◆———

Q. What two cities are connected by the Jim L. Gillis Highway (I-16)?

A. Macon and Savannah.

Q. Where was the first black Muslim sect established in the state?

A. Augusta.

Q. What was the name of the fortification established on St. Simons Island in 1735 by General James E. Oglethorpe?

A. Fort Frederica.

Q. Where was National Baseball Hall of Fame member Ty Cobb born?

A. The Narrows in Banks County.

Q. What building is crowned by the world's largest copper dome?

A. City Auditorium, Macon.

Q. Where was the first Confederate flag raised in the state?

A. Preston, March 31, 1861.

Q. Sandersville is called by what nickname?

A. Kaolin Center of the World.

Q. The ill-fated 1526 Spanish colony of San Miguel de Gualdape was probably located where?

A. At Sapelo Sound in McIntosh County.

Q. What is the largest undeveloped island on the Atlantic Coast?

A. Cumberland.

◆

Q. Mountain View in Clay County was originally known by what name?

A. Rough and Ready.

◆

Q. Who once owned a large plantation at Richmond Hill on the Ogeechee River?

A. Industrialist Henry Ford.

◆

Q. Counties in the state of Georgia are subdivided into political divisions known by what name?

A. Militia districts.

◆

Q. Where was American civil rights leader Martin Luther King, Jr., born?

A. Atlanta.

◆

Q. Where in the state is the oldest congregation in the United States practicing Reform Judaism?

A. Savannah, Mickvi Israel Temple.

◆

Q. The upper tributary of Hannahatchee Creek in Stewart County was given what name by surveyor John G. Scruggs on December 25, 1825?

A. Christmas Branch.

Q. In 1951 Atlanta annexed how many square miles of surrounding land to raise its population by 100,000?

A. Eighty-one.

———◆———

Q. What was the original name of Savannah State College?

A. The Georgia State Industrial College for Colored Youths (1890).

———◆———

Q. The largest computer-controlled railroad classification yard in North America is in what community?

A. Waycross.

———◆———

Q. What was the actual name of the Confederate prison camp at Andersonville?

A. Camp Sumpter.

———◆———

Q. What two lakes does Georgia share with the neighboring state of South Carolina?

A. Hartwell and Clark Hill.

———◆———

Q. Where can the largest peanut in the world be seen?

A. Ashburn.

———◆———

Q. Dade County occupies what corner of the state?

A. Northwest.

Q. Where does Georgia rank in size among the other states?

A. Twenty-first.

———◆———

Q. Built in 1808, what navigational beacon, blown up by Confederate troops in 1862 and rebuilt in 1872, is still in use today?

A. St. Simons Lighthouse.

———◆———

Q. Where is the National Pecan Festival held each year?

A. Albany.

———◆———

Q. The beautiful plantation home of Martha Berry, adjacent to the campus of Berry College near Rome, is known by what name?

A. Oak Hill.

———◆———

Q. Hartsfield Atlanta International Airport was first known by what name?

A. Candler Field.

———◆———

Q. Where can you see a one-of-a-kind double-barreled cannon, designed in 1863 to fire two balls connected by a chain?

A. Athens.

———◆———

Q. Near what town can you find the 1886 Lowery Covered Bridge?

A. Calhoun.

Q. What is the smallest county in area in the state?

A. Clarke.

———◆———

Q. The world's largest manmade beach is claimed by what private lake east of Jonesboro?

A. Lake Spivey.

———◆———

Q. Bricks were brought from what city to construct Albany's first brick house in 1860?

A. Macon.

———◆———

Q. The United States Sixth District headquarters for what federal agency is in Atlanta?

A. The Federal Reserve Bank.

———◆———

Q. The county seat of Jones County is named in honor of what large financier of the Confederacy?

A. James Madison Gray.

———◆———

Q. Which Georgia city is referred to as the Emerald City?

A. Dublin.

———◆———

Q. About how many cities, towns, and villages does Georgia have?

A. 575.

Q. In what town is the University of Georgia?

A. Athens.

◆

Q. For whom was Georgia named?

A. King George II of England.

◆

Q. What Decatur County town is named in honor of the naval officer who commanded the USS *Constitution?*

A. Bainbridge, in honor of William Bainbridge.

◆

Q. Where did President Franklin D. Roosevelt establish his Little White House?

A. Warm Springs.

◆

Q. What is the only Georgia county named for a woman?

A. Hart County, for Revolutionary War heroine Nancy Hart.

◆

Q. In what town is the Sorghum Festival held?

A. Blairsville.

◆

Q. Waycross is the home of a huge railcar repair facility for which railroad line?

A. Seaboard Coastline Railroad.

Q. The famous Calloway Gardens resort is in what county?

A. Harris.

———◆———

Q. What was the peak percentage of black population reached in the state in 1880?

A. 47 percent.

———◆———

Q. What facility in Americus housed thousands of Confederate soldiers as patients between August and December of 1864?

A. Foard Hospital.

———◆———

Q. What section of the state is referred to colloquially as "red land"?

A. North Georgia.

———◆———

Q. In Cornelia, what honors the area's apple growing industry?

A. The Big Red Apple Monument.

———◆———

Q. Near what town is the Old Wooden Jail in which Aaron Burr was incarcerated in 1807 while en route to Virginia to stand trial for treason?

A. Sandersville.

———◆———

Q. What port city is known as the Shrimp Capital of the World?

A. Brunswick.

Q. What community in Echols County received its name from some critical customers of a general store?

A. Needmore.

Q. Where in Georgia did the infamous Trail of Tears begin for the relocation of the Cherokee to western territories?

A. Red Clay.

Q. Who became governor of the state in 1991?

A. Zell Miller.

Q. How does Georgia rank in land area compared with the other states east of the Mississippi River?

A. Largest.

Q. What is the largest lake in Rabun County?

A. Lake Burton.

Q. Where was the boyhood home of Air Force colonel John H. Casper, commander of the space shuttle Endeavor?

A. Chamblee.

Q. Who was the Atlanta dentist and Confederate army officer for whom Hapeville in Fulton County was named?

A. Dr. Samuel Hape.

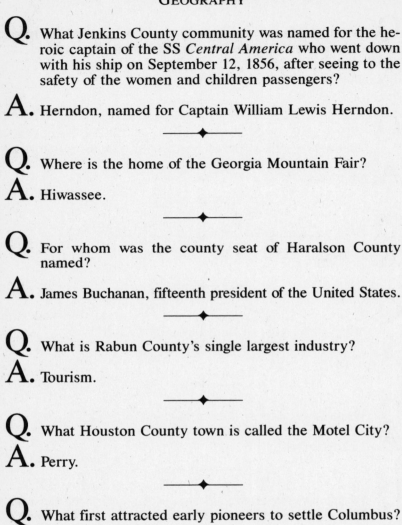

Q. What Jenkins County community was named for the heroic captain of the SS *Central America* who went down with his ship on September 12, 1856, after seeing to the safety of the women and children passengers?

A. Herndon, named for Captain William Lewis Herndon.

Q. Where is the home of the Georgia Mountain Fair?

A. Hiwassee.

Q. For whom was the county seat of Haralson County named?

A. James Buchanan, fifteenth president of the United States.

Q. What is Rabun County's single largest industry?

A. Tourism.

Q. What Houston County town is called the Motel City?

A. Perry.

Q. What first attracted early pioneers to settle Columbus?

A. The Chattahoochee River and its falls.

Q. In what city is the Andrew Low House, home of Juliette Gordon Low, founder of the Girl Scouts?

A. Savannah.

Q. Originally known as Puddleville, a Cook County community changed its name to Adel in 1889 by picking out the four middle letters of what Pennsylvania city?

A. Philadelphia.

———◆———

Q. What is the state motto of Georgia?

A. Wisdom, Justice, and Moderation.

———◆———

Q. What town is called the Watermelon Capital of the World?

A. Cordele.

———◆———

Q. At the start of the Civil War, what percentage of Georgia's population was black?

A. 44 percent.

———◆———

Q. Where is Mule Day held each fall?

A. Calvary.

———◆———

Q. How high is the central mound at the famous Etowah Mound complex near Cartersville?

A. Sixty-five feet.

———◆———

Q. What U.S. military reservation was closed in 1947, only to have a town of the same name incorporated in the same area two years later?

A. Fort Oglethorpe.

Q. Where were live oak timbers cut for use in the construction of the Brooklyn Bridge?

A. Gascoigne Bluff, St. Simons.

◆

Q. What is the greatest distance, east to west, in the state?

A. 250 miles.

◆

Q. Where was the birthplace of Benjamin Harvey Hill, considered to be Jefferson Davis's ablest supporter?

A. Near Hillsboro.

◆

Q. Until 1942, what county could only be entered by way of Alabama or Tennessee?

A. Dade County.

◆

Q. Chickamauga in Walker County was first known by what name?

A. Crawfish Spring.

◆

Q. An early name of Dahlonega was the same as what country?

A. Mexico.

◆

Q. Rutledge is near which state park?

A. Hard Labor Creek State Park.

Q. The Kolomoki Mounds State Park is in what county?

A. Early.

Q. What is the county seat of Brooks County?

A. Quitman.

Q. What is the name of the Civil War cannon manufacturer whose buildings have been renovated into Columbus's Convention and Trade Center?

A. Columbus Iron Works.

Q. How many United States representatives does Georgia have?

A. Eleven.

Q. Where does the southern end of the Appalachian Trail terminate?

A. Springer Mountain.

Q. What do the initials of the FDR school site, located in Seminole County, stand for?

A. The consolidated schools of Fairchild, Desser, and Reynoldsville.

Q. Stone Mountain was named on December 24, 1847, but previous to that it was incorporated under what name?

A. New Gibralter.

Q. Fort Augusta was known by what name during the Revolutionary War?

A. Fort Cornwallis.

———◆———

Q. Brunswick is recognized as a world center for what type of processed food dishes?

A. Seafood dishes.

———◆———

Q. At what city is produced more than half of the world's supply of tufted carpets?

A. Dalton.

———◆———

Q. The name for Hannahatchee Creek in Stewart County is based on what two Muskhogean Indian words?

A. *Achina,* meaning "cedar"; *hachi,* meaning "creek."

———◆———

Q. What was the name of the 10,000-acre estate established in Bartow County just prior to the Civil War by the then wealthiest man in Savannah?

A. Barnsley Gardens.

———◆———

Q. How many senators are there in the state legislature?

A. Fifty-six.

———◆———

Q. In 1868, what city became the capital of the newly reorganized state of Georgia?

A. Atlanta.

Q. What small community, originally known as Wellston, grew to be Georgia's eighth largest city in forty-two short years?

A. Warner Robins.

———◆———

Q. Oxford College at Oxford is a branch of what university?

A. Emory.

———◆———

Q. The Jonquil City is the nickname of what town?

A. Smyrna.

———◆———

Q. The name *Plains* is the shortened form of the name of what older community located about one mile north of the town's present location?

A. Plains of Dura.

———◆———

Q. Where was the last significant land battle of the Civil War fought?

A. Columbus, April 16, 1865.

———◆———

Q. Which town refers to itself as the Poultry Capital of the World?

A. Gainesville.

———◆———

Q. Who serves as president of the Martin Luther King, Jr., Center for Social Change in Atlanta?

A. Coretta Scott King.

Q. What was the name given to the refugee and relocation camp set up by Governor Joseph E. Brown in Dawson following the fall of Atlanta in 1864?

A. Exile Camp.

―――――◆―――――

Q. What is the most southeastern town in the state?

A. St. Marys.

―――――◆―――――

Q. What was the name of the 2,170-acre plantation the legislature of Georgia gave to Revolutionary War hero Major Nathanael Greene?

A. Mulberry Grove.

―――――◆―――――

Q. Adamsville, which has been absorbed by Atlanta, was originally known by what name?

A. Lick Skillet.

―――――◆―――――

Q. How many electoral votes does Georgia have?

A. Thirteen.

―――――◆―――――

Q. Which county is known as the Empire County of the Empire State of the South?

A. Crisp.

―――――◆―――――

Q. How did Newborn, in Newton County, receive its name?

A. Inhabitants wanted their town "born anew" after hearing sermons from the famous evangelist Sam P. Jones.

ENTERTAINMENT

C H A P T E R   T W O

Q. Six Flags Over Georgia covers how many acres?

A. 331 acres.

◆

Q. In which community is the Million Pines Festival held?

A. Soperton.

◆

Q. What famous gospel music quartet worked out of Atlanta from 1948 until 1974?

A. The Statesmen with Hovie Lister.

◆

Q. Atlanta-born actor DeForrest Kelley gained fame playing what character in the "Star Trek" series?

A. Dr. Leonard ("Bones") McCoy.

◆

Q. What 1974 movie filmed in Georgia takes an imprisoned football star and turns him into a coach of the prison football team?

A. *The Longest Yard.*

Q. What actress, who starred in the film *Broadcast News,* was born in Conyers in 1958?

A. Holly Hunter.

———◆———

Q. What festival is held in early April in Sylvania?

A. The Livestock Festival.

———◆———

Q. What television movie starring June Carter Cash, Johnny Cash, and Andy Griffith took place in one of the state's western counties?

A. *Murder in Coweta County.*

———◆———

Q. Who is the Liveoak Gardens-born singer, instrumentalist, and songwriter who won over Greenwich Village audiences with his unique country folk music in the mid-1960s?

A. Patrick ("Pat") Sky.

———◆———

Q. What is the name of the 1,500-acre amusement resort area near Douglas that features the Jet Star Coaster?

A. Holiday Beach.

———◆———

Q. Who is the Macon-born vocalist noted for her passionate southern soul music?

A. Randy Crawford.

———◆———

Q. Who was the nationally famous toothless, raspy-voiced, black comedienne who was born in Brevard in 1897?

A. Moms Mabley.

Q. What television personality born in Nelson starred in several television shows, including "B. J. and the Bear"?

A. Claude Akins.

———◆———

Q. What album won Albany-born Ray Charles two Grammy Awards in 1966 for best rhythm and blues?

A. *Crying Time*.

———◆———

Q. What 1989 movie filmed in Atlanta won four Oscars, including Best Picture?

A. *Driving Miss Daisy*.

———◆———

Q. What group of musicians toured the state following the Civil War to raise money for Confederate soldiers?

A. The Atlanta Amateurs.

———◆———

Q. What is the flagship station for cable giant Turner Communications?

A. WTCG-TV, Channel 17, Atlanta.

———◆———

Q. The country music performing Forester Sisters are from what Georgia community?

A. Lookout Mountain.

———◆———

Q. What country music singer, guitarist, and songwriter was born on June 8, 1932, in Tennga?

A. Clyde Beavers.

Q. What drive-in in Atlanta has the distinction of being the largest in the world?

A. The Varsity.

Q. *Roots,* filmed for television in part in and around Savannah, was a dramatization based on the book by what author?

A. Alex Haley.

Q. What Easter festivity is held on Jekyll Island?

A. The Great Golden Easter Egg Hunt.

Q. What professional football-player-turned-actor was born on St. Simons Island and appeared in such films as *The Dirty Dozen* (1967)?

A. Jim Brown.

Q. Noted female country and western bassist and songwriter Kitty Wilson was born in which Georgia town?

A. Rome.

Q. Where was Otis Redding born on September 9, 1941?

A. Dawson.

Q. What Atlanta outdoor amphitheater hosts events from May through September featuring the symphony, jazz concerts, and popular performers such as James Brown and Dionne Warwick?

A. Chastain Park.

Q. Who from Canton helped pioneer television commercial jingles with tunes for hair care products like Wildroot Cream Oil and White Rain Shampoo?

A. Lee Roy Abernathy

———◆———

Q. How many episodes of "The Dukes of Hazzard" were shot in Georgia in 1979?

A. Five.

———◆———

Q. Neva Jane Langley won what title while representing Georgia in 1953?

A. Miss America.

———◆———

Q. What was Augusta native James Brown's first record release?

A. *Please, Please, Please,* 1956.

———◆———

Q. What actor, born in Waycross in 1891, was married to actress Esther Howard and appeared in *The Argyle Case?*

A. Arthur W. Albertson.

———◆———

Q. What southern action drama, shot in Georgia, starred Burt Reynolds and was a sequel to *White Lightning?*

A. *Gator.*

———◆———

Q. What innovative station break technique was introduced by WSB radio, Atlanta?

A. The use of musical station identification call letters.

Q. What jazz and blues singer born in Cordele sang with Count Basie's Orchestra from 1954 to 1961?

A. Joe Williams.

———◆———

Q. The character Adam on "Bonanza" was played by what Waycross-born actor?

A. Pernell Roberts.

———◆———

Q. Filmed entirely in central Georgia, what TV movie was a dramatization of the 1931 civil rights case involving nine Alabama black men accused of raping two white women?

A. *Judge Horton and the Scottsboro Boys.*

———◆———

Q. What is distinctive about the Scream Machine at Six Flags Over Georgia?

A. It is the longest and tallest wooden roller coaster in the world.

———◆———

Q. Where was Grand Ole Opry member Roy Drusky born on June 22, 1930?

A. Atlanta.

———◆———

Q. Ellijay is the site of what fall festival?

A. The Apple Festival.

———◆———

Q. What black opera singer, born in Atlanta in 1925, toured extensively in Europe?

A. Mattiwilda Dobbs.

Q. In the early 1940s, what gospel group was sponsored on the radio in Atlanta by the SunCrest Bottling Company?

A. The LeFevres.

———◆———

Q. Black actress/director Osceola Archer was born in what Georgia city?

A. Albany.

———◆———

Q. What amusement park is near Rossville?

A. Lake Winnepesaukah Amusement Park.

———◆———

Q. What Albany-born trumpet player and band leader gained national fame while playing two years for Benny Goodman?

A. Harry Haag James.

———◆———

Q. Where can you see Elvis Presley's first limousine?

A. Vintage Auto Museum, Dillard.

———◆———

Q. What group did Atlanta-born jazz musician Edgar W. ("Puddinghead") Battle form at the age of fifteen?

A. The Dixie Serenaders at Morris Brown University.

———◆———

Q. Miniature bell tone rods and amplification produce how many bell sounds for the carillon at Stone Mountain?

A. 732.

Q. What comedy/variety special about great American trains was filmed partly in Georgia and aired on television in 1974?

A. "Johnny Cash Ridin' the Rails."

———◆———

Q. When did the South's first television station, WSB-TV Atlanta, begin operation?

A. 1948.

———◆———

Q. Georgia-born Ray Stevens won a Grammy Award in 1970 for male pop vocalist with what song?

A. "Everything Is Beautiful."

———◆———

Q. What black actor born in Sandersville appeared during the 1970s on such television shows as "The Partridge Family," "Marcus Welby, M.D.," "Streets of San Francisco," and "Columbo"?

A. Herbert Jefferson, Jr.

———◆———

Q. *Scared to Death,* a 1980 film partially produced in Georgia, featured what synthesized genetic organism as the villain creature?

A. Syngenor.

———◆———

Q. What festival celebrates the original European Saint Nicholas Eve?

A. The Sugarplum Festival at Stone Mountain Village.

———◆———

Q. What recording artist born in Atlanta received three gold records for *I'm Sorry, Rocking Around the Christmas Tree,* and *All Alone Am I?*

A. Brenda Lee.

Q. What Fort Benning-born actress appeared in several movies, including *A Shot in the Dark, Dr. Strangelove, Casino Royale, Hammerhead,* and *Car Wash?*

A. Tracy Reed.

———◆———

Q. What was Georgia-born Moms Mabley's actual name?

A. Loretta Mary Aiken.

———◆———

Q. What Whitfield County community hosts the Old Time Fiddlin' Convention each August?

A. Dalton.

———◆———

Q. Where was the Fort Wagner battle scene of the Civil War movie *Glory* filmed?

A. Jekyll Island.

———◆———

Q. What town was the birthplace of actress Joanne Woodward?

A. Thomasville.

———◆———

Q. What musician, composer, and singer born in Atlanta has many hit records including *When You're Hot, You're Hot?*

A. Jerry Reed.

———◆———

Q. The world's only triple-loop roller coaster, at Six Flags Over Georgia, is known by what name?

A. The Mind Bender.

Q. What group had a smash hit in 1973 with its recording of "Midnight Train to Georgia"?

A. Gladys Knight and the Pips.

———◆———

Q. Where was country/western band leader Gid Tanner born in 1885?

A. Near Monroe.

———◆———

Q. The adventures of a black baseball team in the 1940s are portrayed in what Universal film shot in the state?

A. *The Bingo Long Traveling All-Stars and Motor Kings,* 1975–1976.

———◆———

Q. Claudia Coleman, screen, stage, and vaudeville actress of the 1930s, was born in 1889 in what city?

A. Atlanta.

———◆———

Q. What was the name of Roy Drusky's first hit record on the Starday label in 1953?

A. *Such a Fool.*

———◆———

Q. What recording by Dawson-born Otis Redding became number one in the United States and number three in the United Kingdom?

A. "Sittin' on the Dock of the Bay."

———◆———

Q. Which beloved Georgia-born actor, comedian, and recording artist appeared in numerous commercials and is best known for being the voice of Walt Disney's Winnie the Pooh and the narrator of *The Jungle Book*?

A. Sterling Holloway.

Q. What was the name of Pete Drake's group that worked out of Atlanta in the 1950s?

A. Sons of the South.

◆

Q. What made-for-television miniseries was filmed in Georgia in 1974 to help celebrate the Bicentennial?

A. *Give Me Liberty.*

◆

Q. The Gold Leaf Festival may be enjoyed each August in what community?

A. Pelham.

◆

Q. Who is the Athens-born guitar player who won five consecutive awards for Best Acoustic Guitarist from *Guitar Player* magazine?

A. Leo Kottke.

◆

Q. What type of programing was pioneered by Atlanta's Turner Broadcasting on June 1, 1980?

A. Twenty-four-hour-a-day news for cable television.

◆

Q. Civil War nurse Marie LaCoste wrote the words to what song?

A. "Somebody's Darling," in Savannah.

◆

Q. What stage, screen, and television actor born in Georgia appeared in *Lolita* in 1962?

A. William E. Greene.

Q. Actor/director/producer Spike Lee was born on March 20, 1957, in what city?

A. Atlanta.

◆

Q. The grandmother of what actress, who was her namesake, derived her name from a Georgia scenic attraction?

A. Tallulah Bankhead (Tallulah Falls).

◆

Q. What black actor born in Tifton appeared in such soap operas as "All My Children," "Search for Tomorrow," and "Guiding Light"?

A. Dino Shorte.

◆

Q. What Monroe-born trumpet player is best known for his work with Charles Mingus?

A. Lonnie Hillyer.

◆

Q. In 1980, a portion of what movie starring Kurt Russell in the character of Snake Plissken was shot in Georgia?

A. *Escape from New York.*

◆

Q. What Georgia-born baseball star appeared in *The Ninth Inning,* 1942, and *Angels in the Outfield,* 1951?

A. Ty Cobb.

◆

Q. Lou McGarity, trombonist and singer who toured with Bob Crosby in 1964 and in 1967 became a charter member of the World's Greatest Jazz Band, was born in what Georgia community?

A. Athens.

Q. In 1986, Ted Turner acquired MGM/UA for what price?

A. $1.4 billion.

———◆———

Q. What Savannah-born screen, stage, radio, and television actor appeared in many motion pictures, including *The More the Merrier,* 1943, and *Gentlemen Prefer Blondes,* 1953?

A. Charles Douville Coburn.

———◆———

Q. In which month is the Thomasville Rose Festival usually held?

A. April.

———◆———

Q. What actor played detective Allan Pinkerton in the 1990 television drama filmed in Savannah *The Rose and the Jackal?*

A. Christopher Reeve.

———◆———

Q. Georgia-born rhythm and blues singer Willie Jackson won what coveted award in 1973?

A. *Cashbox* Best Female Rhythm and Blues Vocalist.

———◆———

Q. What great comedian was born in Harlem, Georgia, on January 18, 1892?

A. Oliver Norvell Hardy of Laurel and Hardy fame.

———◆———

Q. In 1857, what famous winter song was copyrighted by James Lord Pierpont, organist of the Unitarian church in Savannah?

A. "One Horse Open Sleigh," later retitled "Jingle Bells."

Q. What Atlanta resident came to fame with such songs as "You Picked a Fine Time to Leave Me, Lucille" and "The Gambler"?

A. Kenny Rogers.

———◆———

Q. What PBS broadcast journalist was the first black woman admitted to the University of Georgia in 1961?

A. Charlayne Hunter-Gault.

———◆———

Q. What is the name of the authentic steam engine excursion railroad line in Hartwell?

A. The Red Carpet Line.

———◆———

Q. What was the first radio station in the South, established by the *Atlanta Journal* in 1922?

A. WSB.

———◆———

Q. What Waycross-born actor became famous as the lead in the television series "Dan August," 1970–1971?

A. Burt Reynolds.

———◆———

Q. What production for GE Theater, filmed partly in Georgia, was the story of a Detroit family vacationing in the South?

A. *Just an Old Sweet Song,* 1976.

———◆———

Q. The Lewis Family, known nationally as the First Family of Bluegrass-Gospel Music, hails from what Georgia town?

A. Lincolnton.

Q. What entertainer, born in Atlanta, was master of ceremonies for the Miss America pageants from 1956 to 1979?

A. Bert Parks.

◆

Q. What movie was filmed on northeast Georgia's Chattooga River?

A. *Deliverance.*

◆

Q. In 1955, what recording by Georgia-born Little Richard became a million copy bestseller?

A. "Tutti Frutti."

◆

Q. Where is the Marigold Festival held?

A. Winterville.

◆

Q. Macon-born musician Emmett Berry played what instrument with Teddy Wilson, Eddie Heywood, and Count Basie in the 1930s?

A. Trumpet.

◆

Q. What musical event first held in 1885 in Atlanta became an annual event?

A. Fiddler's Convention.

◆

Q. What novel by Erskine Caldwell, born in White Oak, was turned into a Broadway play and ran for more than seven years?

A. *Tobacco Road.*

Q. Actress Gracie Maldell ("Georgia") Burk, whose career covered radio, television, movies, and theater, was born in 1906 in what town?

A. La Grange.

———◆———

Q. What Walt Disney production was filmed in part in Georgia in 1977?

A. *Million Dollar Dixie Deliverance*.

———◆———

Q. What was the actual name of Ma Rainey, who was born in Columbus in 1886 and is known as the Mother of the Blues?

A. Gertrude Malissa Nix Pridgett.

———◆———

Q. What real estate did Athens-born actress Kim Basinger buy in 1989?

A. The northeast Georgia town Braselton, for twenty million dollars.

———◆———

Q. The annual Heritage Holidays are held in which community?

A. Rome.

———◆———

Q. What film, produced in 1979 and filmed in part in Georgia, is based on a novel by Flannery O'Connor?

A. *Wise Blood*.

———◆———

Q. In what town was the well-known actor Sterling Holloway born?

A. Cedartown.

Q. What famous Savannah composer was widely known for such hits as "Come Rain or Come Shine" and "That Old Black Magic"?

A. Johnny Mercer.

———◆———

Q. In 1952 what Atlanta-born singer won Ted Mack's Amateur Hour at the age of eight?

A. Gladys Knight.

———◆———

Q. Known as one of the most original and forceful trombone soloists of the swing era, what jazz artist hailed from Social Circle, Georgia?

A. Jack ("J. C.") Higginbotham.

———◆———

Q. In what year was the movie *Gone with the Wind* released?

A. 1939.

———◆———

Q. What Savannah-born actor, director, producer, and writer is best known for starring in Mickey Spillane's "Mike Hammer" television show?

A. Stacy Keach, Jr.

———◆———

Q. In what year did Albany-born trumpeter Harry James form his first band?

A. 1939.

———◆———

Q. Where in Emanuel County is the Pine Tree Festival held?

A. Swainsboro.

Q. Where was black comedian Nipsey Russell born?

A. Atlanta.

◆

Q. The Stovall Covered Bridge, built in 1895 near Helen, was featured in what movie?

A. *I'd Climb the Highest Mountain.*

◆

Q. What is the full name of Little Richard?

A. Richard Penniman.

◆

Q. What western movie shot in Georgia in 1979, dealing with the famous James and Younger bank raid in Northfield, Minnesota, starred the Carradine and Keach brothers?

A. *The Long Riders.*

◆

Q. Where is the country music Top of Georgia Jamboree held?

A. Rabun Gap Elementary School, Dillard.

◆

Q. Pop/gospel superstar Amy Grant was born in Augusta on what date?

A. November 25, 1960.

◆

Q. Georgia's film industry is monitored by what state department?

A. Georgia Department of Industry and Trade.

Q. What is the name of Ray Charles's own record label?

A. Tangerine Records.

————◆————

Q. What Academy Award-winning actress once lived in the community of Carrollton?

A. Susan Hayward.

————◆————

Q. Eli Robinson, a veteran of Count Basie's band, was born in which Georgia community?

A. Greenville.

————◆————

Q. Actor Demond Wilson of "Sanford and Son" fame was born in what South Georgia town?

A. Valdosta.

————◆————

Q. Georgia resident Jim Fowler was the long-time co-host and then host of which television series?

A. Mutual of Omaha's "Wild Kingdom."

————◆————

Q. What Marietta country singer became the youngest member of "The Grand Ole Opry" in 1992?

A. James Travis Tritt.

————◆————

Q. What revenge-of-nature science-fiction film featuring man-eating worms was shot in Georgia in 1975?

A. *Squirm.*

Q. What Georgia-born pro football player in the 1970s made numerous commercials, television guest appearances, and appeared in such movies as *In Cold Blood, The Liberation of L. B. Jones* and *Skyjacked?*

A. Roosevelt ("Rosey") Grier.

◆

Q. What was the name of the first successful black musical and comedy troupe?

A. The Georgia Minstrels.

◆

Q. The Trout Festival is held each spring in which community?

A. Dahlonega.

◆

Q. Who starred in the 1981 made-for-television movie *Coward of the County* and had a hit recording of the same title?

A. Georgia-born Kenny Rogers.

◆

Q. What world's leading exponent of bottleneck slide guitar was killed in a motorcycle accident in Macon in 1971?

A. Duane Allman of the Allman Brothers Band.

◆

Q. What single and album went gold for Joe South in 1969?

A. "Games People Play."

◆

Q. Where was Little Richard born?

A. Macon (December 25, 1932).

Q. What Waycross-born musician has toured with such jazz greats as Count Basie, Dizzy Gillespie, Paul Williams, and Aretha Franklin?

A. Daniel William ("Danny") Moore.

———◆———

Q. Each May, Brunswick is the site of what festival?

A. The Brunswick Golden Isles Spring Fiesta.

———◆———

Q. What Atlanta-born guitarist was propelled into national recognition with his recording of "Talking Steel Guitar"?

A. Pete Drake.

———◆———

Q. Larry Fishburne, whose acting credits include *Boyz in the Hood,* was born in what Georgia city in 1962?

A. Augusta.

———◆———

Q. With *Georgia, Georgia* in 1972, who became the first American black woman to have a movie script produced?

A. Maya Angelou.

———◆———

Q. Where are the fall Oktoberfest and winter Fasching Masquerade Karnival held?

A. Helen.

———◆———

Q. Cartersville is the birthplace of what noted hootenanny-era folk singer?

A. Hedy West.

Q. Best known for his originality on the flute, what Savannah-born composer played with Dizzy Gillespie in the 1940s and early 1960s?

A. James Moody.

———◆———

Q. NBC Night at the Movies presented *The Greatest Gift,* filmed partly in Georgia, as a pilot for "The Family Holvak" series starring what actor as the Reverend Holvak?

A. Glenn Ford.

———◆———

Q. What TV actress, born in Decatur on April 23, 1957, appeared on "Saturday Night Live" and "Designing Women"?

A. Jan Hooks.

———◆———

Q. Country music fiddler Clayton ("Pappy") McMichen, born in Allatoona, was noted for forming what Dixieland group?

A. The Georgia Wildcats.

———◆———

Q. What screen, stage, and vaudeville actress, born in Gainesville, appeared in *The Ragamuffin* in 1916?

A. Minnette Barrett.

———◆———

Q. What black actor from Georgia appeared in the 1976 movie *Network*?

A. Author N. Burghardt-Banks.

———◆———

Q. What Savannah-born Louis Armstrong and Jimmy Lunceford soloist appeared on a segment of the TV series "Hawaii Five-O" with Nancy Wilson?

A. James Osborne ("Trummy") Young.

Q. In what town did *Pretty Woman* actress Julia Roberts grow up?

A. Smyrna.

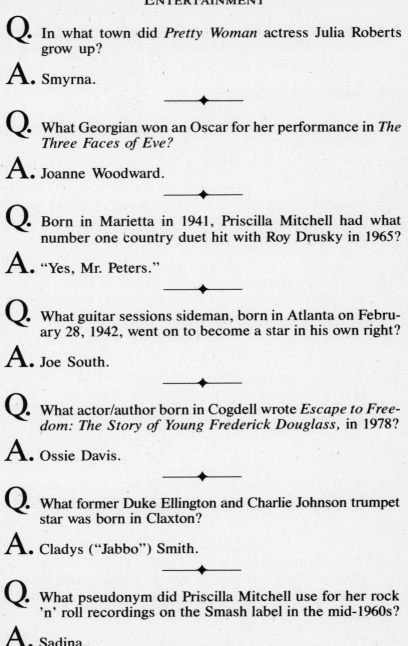

Q. What Georgian won an Oscar for her performance in *The Three Faces of Eve?*

A. Joanne Woodward.

Q. Born in Marietta in 1941, Priscilla Mitchell had what number one country duet hit with Roy Drusky in 1965?

A. "Yes, Mr. Peters."

Q. What guitar sessions sideman, born in Atlanta on February 28, 1942, went on to become a star in his own right?

A. Joe South.

Q. What actor/author born in Cogdell wrote *Escape to Freedom: The Story of Young Frederick Douglass,* in 1978?

A. Ossie Davis.

Q. What former Duke Ellington and Charlie Johnson trumpet star was born in Claxton?

A. Cladys ("Jabbo") Smith.

Q. What pseudonym did Priscilla Mitchell use for her rock 'n' roll recordings on the Smash label in the mid-1960s?

A. Sadina.

Q. What Atlanta-born actor appeared in several movies, including *Fingerprints Don't Lie, Gene Autry and the Mounties,* and *Texans Never Cry,* all in 1951?

A. Royal ("Roy") Butler.

◆

Q. What Georgia-born actress has made it big in such movies as *9½ Weeks* and *Batman?*

A. Kim Basinger.

◆

Q. What was the name of Gid Tanner's early country music group that worked out of Atlanta in the mid-1920s?

A. The Skillet Lickers.

◆

Q. What Savannah-born jazz banjo and guitar player worked with such greats as Jelly Roll Morton and Louis Armstrong in the 1920s and 1930s?

A. Lee L. Blair.

◆

Q. What was the birthplace of black actress Pauline Evelyn Myers, who appeared in *Green Pastures, Tarzan's Flight for Life, Tick . . . Tick . . . Tick,* and *Lady Sings the Blues?*

A. Ocilla.

◆

Q. What historic Chatham County plantation was the location for the 1962 film *Cape Fear,* starring Gregory Peck?

A. Grove Point.

◆

Q. What Covington-born tenor sax player began his career in Georgia and played behind Sam Cooke and Hank Ballard in Atlanta?

A. George Rufus Adams.

HISTORY

CHAPTER THREE

Q. What two young Anglican clergymen came to Georgia in 1735 as missionaries and later founded Methodism?

A. John and Charles Wesley.

———◆———

Q. When were the last Cherokee Indians removed from Georgia?

A. 1838.

———◆———

Q. Jimmy Carter served as president of the United States during what years?

A. 1977–1981.

———◆———

Q. What was the date of the first national holiday in honor of the birthday of Dr. Martin Luther King, Jr.?

A. Monday, January 20, 1986.

———◆———

Q. When did Georgia become a state?

A. January 2, 1788.

Q. Fort Benning, adjoining Columbus, is named for what distinguished Confederate general?

A. Native son Henry L. Benning.

◆

Q. What was the first nuclear-powered merchant vessel?

A. The NS *Savannah*.

◆

Q. What highly decorated air ace of World Wars I and II was a native of Savannah?

A. Major General Frank O'Driscoll Hunter.

◆

Q. Georgia civil rights leader and political activist Julian Bond graduated from what educational institution?

A. Morehouse College.

◆

Q. In what year were women first allowed to practice law in the courts of Georgia?

A. 1915.

◆

Q. What religious group was excluded from the colony of Georgia for fear that its members would spy for the French in Louisiana and the Spanish in Florida?

A. The Roman Catholics.

◆

Q. Born in Cherokee County, who served as secretary of state from 1961 to 1969 under Presidents John F. Kennedy and Lyndon B. Johnson?

A. Dean Rusk.

Q. Where was the first machinists' union in the United States formed?

A. Atlanta, in 1888.

◆

Q. Who was the daring French sailor who explored the coast of Georgia in 1562, seeking to establish a colony of French Huguenots?

A. Jean Ribault.

◆

Q. In 1943 Georgia was the first state to give eighteen-year-olds what privilege?

A. The right to vote.

◆

Q. In the early years of Georgia colonization the manufacturing and sale of what beverage was prohibited?

A. Whiskey (law repealed in 1742).

◆

Q. What was the name of the combined school and orphanage established near Savannah in 1740 that became the most successful charitable and educational endeavor of the colonial period?

A. Bethesda Orphan House.

◆

Q. How much money disappeared from the Confederate treasury in Washington, never to be recovered?

A. $400,000 in gold.

◆

Q. Who was the first European to explore the interior of Georgia?

A. Hernando de Soto, 1540.

Q. The remains of what two Confederate gunboats are on display at the Confederate Naval Museum in Columbus?

A. The CSS *Chattahoochee* and the CSS *Jackson/Muscogee*.

———◆———

Q. Where did Gulf War commander Gen. Norman Schwarzkopf once serve in Georgia?

A. Fort Stewart (he commanded the 24th Infantry Division, 1983–85).

———◆———

Q. What is the name of the site of the Civil War battle that opened the way to Atlanta for General Sherman?

A. Resaca.

———◆———

Q. Who was General James Edward Oglethorpe's native American interpreter?

A. Mary Musgrove.

———◆———

Q. As the Confederacy began to crumble, to whom did Georgia surrender its armies?

A. General James H. Wilson.

———◆———

Q. What was the purpose of the expedition organized in 1559 by Luis de Velasco up the Chattahoochee River into northern Georgia?

A. To establish gold mining operations.

———◆———

Q. Born near Augusta, what Confederate general commanded American forces during the Spanish–American War and in the Philippine insurrection of 1900?

A. Joseph Wheeler.

Q. Where did President Franklin D. Roosevelt die?

A. The Little White House, Warm Springs.

———◆———

Q. What was the name of the organization that first appeared in the state in 1867 to organize black voters?

A. The Loyal or Union League.

———◆———

Q. What is Georgia's oldest independent (non-tax supported) institution of higher education?

A. LaGrange College.

———◆———

Q. What young army officer assisted with the construction of Fort Pulaski?

A. Lt. Robert E. Lee (1829–31).

———◆———

Q. When did the first 120 colonists arrive in Georgia, under the leadership of James Oglethorpe?

A. February 12, 1733.

———◆———

Q. Where did the Presbyterian Church establish Oglethorpe College in 1836?

A. Near Milledgeville.

———◆———

Q. What religious entity was formed in Augusta in May 1845, by seceding from the American Baptist Union over, among other issues, slavery?

A. The Southern Baptist Convention.

Q. Georgia, Kentucky, and Tennessee all claim to be the birthplace of what famous frontiersman who died at the Alamo?

A. James Bowie.

———◆———

Q. Where did Pedro Menéndez de Avilés establish a Spanish garrison in 1566?

A. St. Catherines Island.

———◆———

Q. What religious group established a mission school for Indians at Irene in 1736?

A. The Moravians.

———◆———

Q. What exclusive boarding house in Atlanta in the early 1900s provided young men of considerable means a name in society?

A. The Bell House (Bell House "boys").

———◆———

Q. What property was stolen from the Presbyterian Church in Madison during the Civil War, later to be returned by Federal orders?

A. The church's silver communion service.

———◆———

Q. What U.S. Supreme Court justice was born in Savannah on June 23, 1948?

A. Clarence Thomas.

———◆———

Q. What was the name of the first iron sea vessel, built in Savannah?

A. The *John Randolph,* 1834.

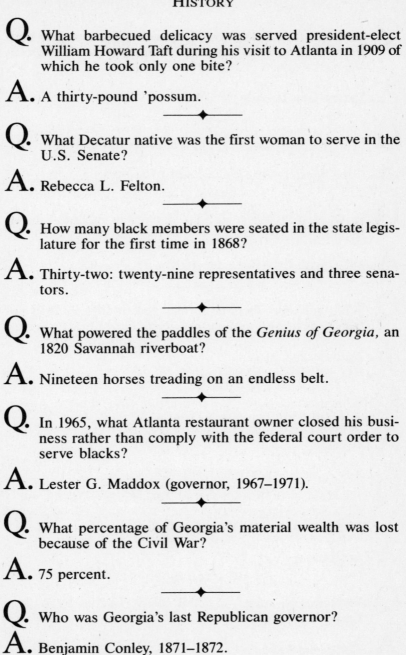

Q. What barbecued delicacy was served president-elect William Howard Taft during his visit to Atlanta in 1909 of which he took only one bite?

A. A thirty-pound 'possum.

———◆———

Q. What Decatur native was the first woman to serve in the U.S. Senate?

A. Rebecca L. Felton.

———◆———

Q. How many black members were seated in the state legislature for the first time in 1868?

A. Thirty-two: twenty-nine representatives and three senators.

———◆———

Q. What powered the paddles of the *Genius of Georgia,* an 1820 Savannah riverboat?

A. Nineteen horses treading on an endless belt.

———◆———

Q. In 1965, what Atlanta restaurant owner closed his business rather than comply with the federal court order to serve blacks?

A. Lester G. Maddox (governor, 1967–1971).

———◆———

Q. What percentage of Georgia's material wealth was lost because of the Civil War?

A. 75 percent.

———◆———

Q. Who was Georgia's last Republican governor?

A. Benjamin Conley, 1871–1872.

Q. Who was the modest young Spanish–American War hero from Marietta who served as Admiral Dewey's flag officer at the battle of Manila?

A. Lieutenant Thomas M. Brumby.

◆

Q. Which was the last Confederate fort to fall?

A. Fort Tyler, Troup County, April 16, 1865.

◆

Q. In what year was telephone service inaugurated in Atlanta?

A. 1879, with fifty-five subscribers.

◆

Q. Who built Fort Deposit in Dawson County in 1818 primarily as a food and supplies depot?

A. Andrew Jackson.

◆

Q. What city was known at one time as the smallest American city with a streetcar system?

A. Valdosta.

◆

Q. What social studies teacher at Fort Valley's Peach County High School has written a series of campaign histories and tour guides of Civil War battlefields?

A. Jim Miles.

◆

Q. Numerically, what president of the United States was Jimmy Carter?

A. Thirty-ninth.

Q. When was the capitol dedicated in Atlanta?

A. July 4, 1889.

———◆———

Q. How many immigrants arrived in Georgia between 1732 and 1740?

A. 2,500.

———◆———

Q. The U.S. Congress authorized the minting of a commemorative half dollar in connection with what Civil War memorial project?

A. The Stone Mountain Memorial, 1925.

———◆———

Q. Under whose leadership did the Ku Klux Klan begin to operate in the state in the spring of 1868?

A. General John B. Gordon.

———◆———

Q. Where in Wilkes County was the Confederate cabinet dissolved and the Southern army disbanded?

A. Washington.

———◆———

Q. In what year did Georgia establish its first public school system?

A. 1870.

———◆———

Q. Who accompanied the original settlers and became the first teacher in the colony of Georgia?

A. Reverend Benjamin Ingham.

Q. Whose election as mayor of Atlanta in 1973 made him the first black mayor of a major southern city?

A. Maynard H. Jackson, Jr.

———◆———

Q. What world famous aviator visited Southern Airfield in Americus in 1923 to purchase and fly solo a "Jenny" airplane?

A. Charles A. Lindbergh.

———◆———

Q. What means of mass transit was established in Atlanta in 1871?

A. Horse-drawn streetcars.

———◆———

Q. What U.S. legislation was enacted due to the efforts of Georgia to overturn a 1793 Supreme Court ruling allowing individuals to sue states?

A. The Eleventh Amendment to the U.S. Constitution, 1798.

———◆———

Q. In 1804, what town became the site of the state capital?

A. Milledgeville.

———◆———

Q. Where in Georgia did Lutheran immigrants establish two schools in 1734, in which German was the principal language for more than fifty years?

A. Ebenezer.

———◆———

Q. In what year was Coca-Cola first made?

A. 1886.

Q. What Georgia Democrat was the first African American elected to Congress from the South since 1901 and the first black man to serve as U.S. ambassador to the United Nations?

A. Andrew Jackson Young, Jr.

Q. Who built the first steamboat in Georgia in 1807, shortly after Robert Fulton's *Clermont* had been launched?

A. William Longstreet of Augusta.

Q. Georgia became the first state to extend what rights to married women?

A. Full property rights, 1866.

Q. When did Georgia secede from the Union?

A. January 19, 1861.

Q. For what was the penitentiary at Milledgeville utilized during the Civil War?

A. An armory.

Q. What was the first state-owned railroad in the United States created by the Georgia General Assembly on December 21, 1836?

A. The Western and Atlantic Railroad.

Q. In 1893 Thomas E. Watson introduced a bill in the U.S. Congress that created what public service?

A. Rural free mail delivery.

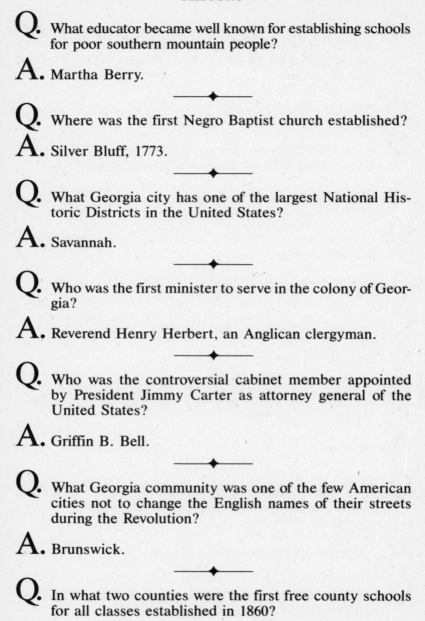

Q. What educator became well known for establishing schools for poor southern mountain people?

A. Martha Berry.

Q. Where was the first Negro Baptist church established?

A. Silver Bluff, 1773.

Q. What Georgia city has one of the largest National Historic Districts in the United States?

A. Savannah.

Q. Who was the first minister to serve in the colony of Georgia?

A. Reverend Henry Herbert, an Anglican clergyman.

Q. Who was the controversial cabinet member appointed by President Jimmy Carter as attorney general of the United States?

A. Griffin B. Bell.

Q. What Georgia community was one of the few American cities not to change the English names of their streets during the Revolution?

A. Brunswick.

Q. In what two counties were the first free county schools for all classes established in 1860?

A. Gordon and Gilmer counties.

Q. Action by the Georgia legislature revoking some land grants led to what 1810 U.S. Supreme Court decision, for the first time declaring a state law unconstitutional?

A. *Fletcher* v. *Peck.*

———◆———

Q. What building served as the first statehouse in Atlanta?

A. The Atlanta City Hall, Fulton County Courthouse.

———◆———

Q. How many troops did Georgia provide for the Confederate cause during the four years of the Civil War?

A. Nearly 125,000.

———◆———

Q. What was the name of the one-way shallow wooden barges used to ship cotton downriver to market towns?

A. Cottonboxes.

———◆———

Q. The oldest Baptist church in Georgia, the Old Kiokee Baptist Church near Appling, was established in what year?

A. 1771.

———◆———

Q. In 1749 the law prohibiting what practice in the Georgia colony was repealed?

A. Slaveholding.

———◆———

Q. Where was the Battle of Bloody Marsh, in which the English scored a decisive victory over the Spanish, fought on July 7, 1742?

A. St. Simons Island.

Q. The city of Perry is named for what naval hero?

A. Commodore Oliver Hazard Perry.

---◆---

Q. The Vann House, situated near Chatsworth, holds what distinction?

A. It is the only mansion in America built by a native American, Chief Joseph Vann.

---◆---

Q. Who is known as the father of Georgia's public school system?

A. Gustavus J. Orr.

---◆---

Q. What was the name of the Cherokee capital in Gordon County?

A. New Echota.

---◆---

Q. What does the ship on the reverse side of the state seal represent?

A. Georgia's exports.

---◆---

Q. How did Georgia congressman Rufus E. Lester die in Washington, D.C., in 1906?

A. By falling through a hotel skylight.

---◆---

Q. What controversial revenue measure was narrowly approved by Georgia voters in 1992?

A. A lottery.

Q. What historic home in Macon was built in 1853 by Judge Asa Holt?

A. The Old Cannonball House.

———◆———

Q. Who was the French black man who founded a school in Savannah for free black children in 1818?

A. Julian Froumontaine.

———◆———

Q. A U.S. senator since 1972, what Georgian heads the powerful Armed Services Committee?

A. Sam Nunn.

———◆———

Q. What educational institution was established in the old state capitol at Milledgeville in 1879?

A. Georgia Military College.

———◆———

Q. What were the three requirements issued by President Andrew Johnson for Georgia to be readmitted to the Union?

A. The emancipation of slaves, repudiation of Confederate war debts, and repeal of secession ordinances.

———◆———

Q. What exposition was held in 1881 that brought national attention to Atlanta as a manufacturing, distribution, and transportation center?

A. The International Cotton Exposition.

———◆———

Q. Where was the largest sawmill in the South established in the mid-1800s?

A. Lumber City, Telfair County.

Q. When did the nation's first gold rush occur?

A. 1828, around Dahlonega.

Q. By what nickname was the Revolutionary War general Francis Marion, for whom Marion County was named, known?

A. Swamp Fox.

Q. What Marietta-born soldier served as commander in chief of the U.S. armed forces in Europe and as military governor of the American zone in Germany from 1947 to 1949?

A. Lucius D. Clay.

Q. What facility at the state sanitorium, Milledgeville, now named Central State Hospital, is the largest of its kind in the world?

A. The world's largest kitchen, capable of preparing approximately 30,000 meals a day.

Q. What was the name of a woolen cloth produced in Georgia in the 1830s to compete with English imports?

A. Georgia Plains.

Q. In what Georgia community was the first kindergarten in the United States established?

A. Madison.

Q. In 1929, who presented to Rome, Georgia, the Capitoline Wolf, a bronze replica of the statue of Romulus and Remus and their she-wolf nurse?

A. Benito Mussolini.

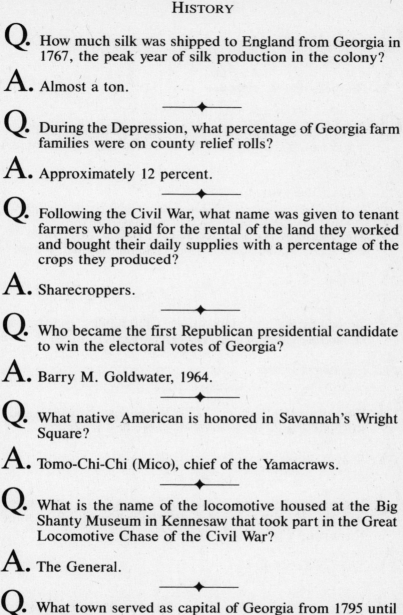

Q. How much silk was shipped to England from Georgia in 1767, the peak year of silk production in the colony?

A. Almost a ton.

———◆———

Q. During the Depression, what percentage of Georgia farm families were on county relief rolls?

A. Approximately 12 percent.

———◆———

Q. Following the Civil War, what name was given to tenant farmers who paid for the rental of the land they worked and bought their daily supplies with a percentage of the crops they produced?

A. Sharecroppers.

———◆———

Q. Who became the first Republican presidential candidate to win the electoral votes of Georgia?

A. Barry M. Goldwater, 1964.

———◆———

Q. What native American is honored in Savannah's Wright Square?

A. Tomo-Chi-Chi (Mico), chief of the Yamacraws.

———◆———

Q. What is the name of the locomotive housed at the Big Shanty Museum in Kennesaw that took part in the Great Locomotive Chase of the Civil War?

A. The General.

———◆———

Q. What town served as capital of Georgia from 1795 until 1804?

A. Louisville.

Q. Charles Wesley served in what capacity for James Oglethorpe?

A. His personal secretary.

———◆———

Q. What name was given to the 1,400-acre interracial commune established in 1942 by Clarence Jordon in Sumter County?

A. Koinonia Farms.

———◆———

Q. The Marietta National Cemetery contains the graves of how many Union soldiers from General Sherman's army?

A. 10,000.

———◆———

Q. To whom did the state grant a monopoly in 1814 for steam navigation on all Georgia streams?

A. Samuel Howard.

———◆———

Q. Who was the famous 1890s evangelist whose home, Roselawn, may be seen in Cartersville?

A. Sam P. Jones.

———◆———

Q. What was the name of the first steamship to cross the Atlantic in 1819, owned and operated by the Savannah Steamship Company?

A. The SS *Savannah*.

———◆———

Q. What was the actual name of the notorious pirate for whom Blackbeard Island is named?

A. Edward Teach.

Q. What was the name of the ship on which the first colonists of Georgia arrived?

A. *Anne.*

———◆———

Q. The ambitious sculpturing project on Stone Mountain begun in 1923 was completed in what year?

A. 1969.

———◆———

Q. What acting governor of Georgia (in 1777) was later killed in a duel by General Lachlan McIntosh because of rivalry for the post of brigadier general of troops raised in Georgia?

A. Button Gwinnett.

———◆———

Q. Walter F. George, born near Preston, was appointed by President Dwight D. Eisenhower to what ambassadorship?

A. North Atlantic Treaty Organization (NATO).

———◆———

Q. What legislation on education was enacted in 1916?

A. Compulsory school law.

———◆———

Q. What action was taken against Georgia in 1867 for refusing to ratify the Fourteenth Amendment giving African Americans full citizenship?

A. Congress placed Georgia under military rule.

———◆———

Q. In the 1980s and 1990s what Georgian served several terms as minority whip in the U.S. House of Representatives?

A. Newt Gingrich.

Q. Richmond Academy, the first free government-supported high school, was established in what city?

A. Augusta, 1783.

Q. What Georgian was the recipient of the 1964 Nobel Peace Prize?

A. Dr. Martin Luther King, Jr.

Q. What Christmas present did General Sherman give President Lincoln in 1864?

A. The city of Savannah, which he had just captured.

Q. What fort did Governor Joseph E. Brown order occupied by state troops sixteen days prior to the state's secession from the Union?

A. Fort Pulaski, near Savannah.

Q. What organization formed in 1867 was instrumental in persuading the legislature to pass adequate educational laws?

A. The State Teachers Association.

Q. Who were the two major Indian tribes in Georgia in colonial days?

A. Creek and Cherokee.

Q. How much money was appropriated in 1883 by the state legislature for the construction of the capitol in Atlanta?

A. $1 million.

Q. Who was the notorious Reconstruction-era governor who eventually resigned and fled the state?

A. Rufus Bullock, 1868–1870.

———◆———

Q. Who originally planned the city of Brunswick?

A. General James E. Oglethorpe.

———◆———

Q. What friendly agricultural people of the Creek tribe are honored by a monument near Leesburg?

A. The Chehaw Indians.

———◆———

Q. Where was the first experimental five-mile strip of concrete highway constructed in the state in 1919?

A. North of Griffin.

———◆———

Q. Georgia State University of Atlanta evolved from what educational facility founded in 1913?

A. Georgia Tech Evening School of Commerce.

———◆———

Q. In 1888, what Richmond, Virginia, physician gave Georgia its first free library?

A. Francis T. Willis (the Mary Willis Free Library in Washington).

———◆———

Q. What famous document did Georgians Button Gwinnett, Lyman Hall, and George Walton sign?

A. The Declaration of Independence.

Q. The mother of which U.S. president spent her girlhood days at Roswell?

A. Theodore Roosevelt.

◆

Q. In 1788 Alexander Bissell of St. Simons Island was the first person to export what product to England?

A. Cotton.

◆

Q. Which governor was called "the one-eyed plowboy from Pigeon Roost"?

A. Allen Daniel Candler, 1898–1902.

◆

Q. What former coastal defense fortress located on Cockspur Island was declared a national monument in 1924?

A. Fort Pulaski.

◆

Q. What was the name of the first brewery built in the state, used to supply ale to troops and settlers at Fort Frederica?

A. Horton's Brewery.

◆

Q. What was the nature of the resolution passed by the legislature of South Carolina in the fall of 1776 and presented to the lawmakers of Georgia?

A. The proposed merger of the two states.

◆

Q. As a young man, who established and operated an academy for a short time near Eatonton and later purchased Alaska for the United States?

A. William H. Seward.

Q. Who was the first royal governor of Georgia?

A. John Reynolds, 1754–1757.

Q. Red Clay was the last site for what function of the eastern band of the Cherokee Nation?

A. Council grounds.

Q. When was the charter establishing the colony of Georgia signed in England?

A. June 9, 1732.

Q. In the founding of the thirteen original colonies, where did Georgia rank chronologically?

A. Thirteenth.

Q. Who in 1717 first applied the name *Golden Isles* to the coastal islands of the state?

A. Sir Robert Montgomery.

Q. For what sum of money did Asa Griggs Candler, Sr., become the sole owner of Coca-Cola in 1891?

A. $2,300.

Q. Who was the heroic Polish count who was mortally wounded at the siege of Savannah, October 9, 1779?

A. Casimir Pulaski.

Q. As Union forces drew near to Atlanta in June 1864, Governor Brown made a desperate call for recruits who became known by what name?

A. Joe Brown Malish.

――――◆――――

Q. What Georgian organized the first Girl Scout troop in 1912?

A. Juliette Gordon Low.

――――◆――――

Q. Why did Augusta escape the wrath of General Sherman in the Civil War?

A. It is said that he spared the city because he had loved a girl who lived there.

――――◆――――

Q. Georgia Southern College in Statesboro originally opened classes in 1908 under what name?

A. First District Agricultural and Mechanical High School.

――――◆――――

Q. The Atlanta Plantation, which was established in Glynn County in 1815, was purchased by what religious sect in 1898?

A. The Shakers.

――――◆――――

Q. Which professor of economics and history at Atlanta University, 1897–1910, was a leader of social reform on behalf of his fellow blacks?

A. W. E. B. Du Bois.

――――◆――――

Q. What was the name of the short-lived antiblack labor movement that swept across the state in the late summer and fall of 1930?

A. The American Fascisti Association and Order of Black Shirts.

Q. What did Jimmy Carter do to help honor notable black Georgians while he was governor?

A. In 1973 he appointed a committee to nominate blacks for the portrait galleries in the state capitol.

———◆———

Q. What community is considered to be the only surviving example of a complete Federal period city?

A. Milledgeville.

———◆———

Q. What was the name of the first major anti–British organization in the Georgia colony?

A. The Liberty Boys, 1765.

———◆———

Q. The original state constitution in 1777 provided for what type of institutions to "be erected and supported at the general expense of the state" in each county?

A. Schools.

———◆———

Q. How many Union prisoners died at the Confederate POW camp at Andersonville during its fourteen-month existence?

A. More than 12,900.

———◆———

Q. Who was the first Georgia governor elected by popular vote?

A. George Michael Troup, 1823–1827.

———◆———

Q. As a royal province of England, where was Georgia's first capital?

A. Savannah.

Q. At one time Augusta was the largest inland market in the world for what commodity?

A. Cotton.

Q. Spelman College in Atlanta was the first school to grant what type of certificate to a black student?

A. A nursing certificate, 1881.

Q. What took place at the Jekyll Island Club in 1915 that made communication history?

A. The first transcontinental telephone call was made.

Q. During the Franklin Roosevelt administration, Atlanta was selected as the first city to receive government funding for what type of project?

A. Slum clearance.

Q. What three famous Confederate personages are memorialized on Stone Mountain?

A. Jefferson Davis, Robert E. Lee, and Stonewall Jackson.

Q. Who was Georgia's first chief justice?

A. Joseph Henry Lumkin.

Q. Which engagement of Confederate and Union troops is known as the two bloodiest days of the Civil War?

A. The Battle of Chickamauga, September 19–20, 1863.

Q. With what church did the Assembly of Georgia declare official adherence in 1758?

A. The Church of England.

◆

Q. By what name was the acquisition of 35 million acres of Georgia's territory for less than 1½ cents per acre by unscrupulous land companies in 1795 known?

A. The Yazoo Fraud.

◆

Q. What popular story about the origin of the colony of Georgia is largely untrue?

A. The plan to use it as a place to send imprisoned or released debtors was abandoned and few went to Georgia.

◆

Q. A state prohibition law was passed in what year?

A. 1907, repealed in 1938.

◆

Q. What political party has controlled Georgia politics throughout most of the state's history?

A. The Democratic party.

◆

Q. Approximately how many Union soldiers accompanied General Sherman on his March to the Sea?

A. Approximately 60,000.

◆

Q. What president of the United States grew up in Augusta during the Civil War?

A. Woodrow Wilson.

Q. When did General Sherman's army set fire to Atlanta?

A. November 14, 1864.

———◆———

Q. In what year did high schools become a part of the state's public educational system?

A. 1912.

———◆———

Q. What Confederate memorial is situated in Thomson McDuffie County?

A. A monument to Confederate women.

———◆———

Q. Who founded the first Sunday school in the colony of Georgia?

A. The German Lutherans of Ebenezer.

———◆———

Q. Until 1908, what group of people could be leased by the state to private individuals or companies for manual labor?

A. Convicts.

———◆———

Q. The convergence of the Western and Atlantic, the Macon and Western, and the Georgian railroads, which eventually would become the site of present-day Atlanta, was first known by what name?

A. Terminus.

———◆———

Q. For what purpose was Gammon Theological Seminary founded in Atlanta in 1883?

A. The education of black ministers.

Q. Which one of the Golden Isles is named for the Indian word for salt?

A. Tybee Island.

Q. Who were the Nancy Harts?

A. A group of militiawomen organized to defend La Grange during the Civil War.

Q. By what name was the present site of Atlanta known from 1842 to 1845?

A. Marthasville.

Q. Where was the bell cast that was once located in the old market in Louisville?

A. France, 1772.

Q. Where was Jefferson Davis, president of the Confederacy, captured on May 16, 1865?

A. Approximately two miles north of Irwinville.

Q. During what years was Louisville the state capital?

A. 1796–1805.

Q. What act of nature leveled all but one column of the old slave market in Augusta in 1878?

A. A cyclone.

Q. Who were the first Roman Catholics to be admitted into Georgia?

A. Irish Redemptionists who had pledged service for passage to the New World.

----◆----

Q. What emblem of freedom was brought to Atlanta for display in the Cotton States and International Exposition parade of 1895?

A. The Liberty Bell.

----◆----

Q. What event of January 1866 greatly helped foster better educational opportunities for blacks?

A. The formation of a black educational association.

----◆----

Q. In 1916 what department of the state government served as a highway board?

A. The state prison board.

----◆----

Q. During what years did Augusta serve as the state's capital?

A. 1783–1795.

----◆----

Q. In 1906 the legislature enacted a law prohibiting the employment of what segment of the population?

A. Children under ten years of age.

----◆----

Q. What was the name of the Jewish welfare service formed in Atlanta during the Civil War?

A. The Hebrew Benevolent Society.

Q. Who was the Paul Revere of the South, the Rome letter carrier who rode sixty-seven miles to warn the town of approaching Yankees?

A. John Wisdom.

------◆------

Q. What was the annual salary approved in 1743 by the common council of Savannah for a teacher to serve in the city's free school?

A. Twenty pounds sterling.

------◆------

Q. On January 27, 1785, what institution became the first state university to be chartered in America?

A. The University of Georgia.

------◆------

Q. In 1825 Governor George M. Troup declared that a state of war would exist between Georgia and the United States if the federal government did not carry out what process?

A. The removal of Creek Indians from Georgia.

------◆------

Q. In 1836, what college became the first in the world chartered to grant degrees exclusively to women?

A. The Georgia Female College, Macon (renamed Wesleyan College).

------◆------

Q. The Georgian Heritage Celebration recalls what event?

A. The founding of Georgia at Savannah, February 12, 1733.

------◆------

Q. In 1874 Georgia led the nation in establishing what state department?

A. The Georgia Department of Agriculture.

Q. Who was governor of Georgia during the Civil War, the only Georgia governor to serve four terms?

A. Joe E. Brown.

———◆———

Q. Where was the first printed cotton cloth produced in the state?

A. John Shly's textile mill near Augusta, around 1834.

———◆———

Q. In December 1829 the legislature made what activity with blacks illegal?

A. The education of blacks, slave or free.

———◆———

Q. In what year was Georgia readmitted into the Union?

A. 1870.

———◆———

Q. Who is said to have greeted every ship that entered the port of Savannah from 1887 to 1931 and is honored by a statue of a waving girl in Riverfront Plaza?

A. Florence Martus.

———◆———

Q. What U.S. president practiced law in Atlanta as a young man from 1882 to 1883?

A. Woodrow Wilson.

———◆———

Q. What early American explorer, soldier, and political leader born in Savannah was nicknamed the Pathfinder because of his explorations between the Rocky Mountains and the Pacific Ocean?

A. John Charles Frémont.

Q. What year was Atlanta's first full-time police force established?

A. 1873.

Q. What was the dollar amount of the property damage that General Sherman estimated his army cost Georgia?

A. $1 million.

Q. Who was the young lady from Knoxville in Crawford County who designed the famous Lone Star flag of Texas?

A. Joanna E. Troutman.

Q. What man served thirty-four years in the U.S. Senate, never losing an election and having the law school at Mercer University named in his honor?

A. Walter F. George.

Q. What staff officer urged Gen. Robert E. Lee to simply disband his army rather than surrender at Appomattox?

A. Brig. Gen. Edward Porter Alexander of Washington, Georgia.

Q. Who was the noted Methodist churchman who held the first Methodist Conference near Elberton in 1788?

A. Bishop Francis Asbury.

Q. In 1754 Georgia received what status from England?

A. Royal province.

Q. The state constitution of 1877 legitimized what discriminatory practice in education?

A. The segregated school system.

◆

Q. The Old Greene County jail built in 1807 in Greensboro imitates what architectural style?

A. Bastilles of the nineteenth century.

◆

Q. When was an independent highway board created within the state government?

A. 1919.

◆

Q. What Jewish widow from Savannah wrote of being the last representative of the Confederate government to remain at her post after the fall of Richmond in 1865?

A. Phoebe Yates Pember, a matron at Chimborazo Hospital, in *A Southern Woman's Story,* 1879.

◆

Q. What heroic young colonel from Georgia died at Fort Goliad in 1836 during the War of Texas Independence?

A. Colonel James W. Fannin.

◆

Q. Based on Governor James Wright's estimated figures, what was the population of Georgia in 1766?

A. 10,000 whites and 7,800 blacks.

◆

Q. On what date was Atlanta first illuminated by a new gas lighting system?

A. December 25, 1855.

Q. What was the occupation of William Berry Hartsfield, for whom the Hartsfield International Airport in Atlanta was named in 1970?

A. Mayor of Atlanta, 1937–1960.

◆

Q. Small rural elementary schools operating without state or county control in the early nineteenth century were known by what name?

A. Old Field Schools.

◆

Q. In what year did the Creek Indians leave Georgia and move west of the Mississippi River?

A. 1826.

◆

Q. What black preacher, with the aid of Rev. Abraham Marshall, organized the First African Baptist Church in Savannah in 1788?

A. Jesse Peter.

◆

Q. The first Presbyterian colonists who settled at Darien in 1735 were of what ethnic background?

A. Scottish Highlanders.

◆

Q. Who organized the first state fair at Stone Mountain in 1846?

A. The South Central Agricultural Society.

◆

Q. What was the seemingly excessive construction price of an Augusta Federal-style home built in 1818 that led to its being named Ware's Folly?

A. $40,000.

Q. What were the Cherokee Indians offered in 1835 to give up their Georgia holdings?

A. $5 million and relocation in the West.

◆

Q. Who was the governor from 1827 to 1829 who also served as secretary of state under President Van Buren?

A. John Forsyth.

◆

Q. James Hamilton, who established the Hamilton Plantation on St. Simons Island in 1804, was a native of what country?

A. Scotland.

◆

Q. Who was the first Presbyterian evangelist to enter Georgia?

A. Reverend John Newton, in 1785.

◆

Q. What event is reenacted the first Saturday of every December at Old Fort Jackson?

A. The capture of Savannah by General Sherman in 1864.

◆

Q. In 1757 who built Fort Ebenezer, in what became Effingham County, to protect settlers from Indian attacks?

A. John Gerar William DeBrahm.

◆

Q. What community, at one time located across the Ocmulgee River from Hawkinsville, came within one vote of becoming the state capital in 1804?

A. Hartford, in Pulaski County.

ARTS & LITERATURE

CHAPTER FOUR

Q. Who is the internationally recognized Georgia writer known for such works as her St. Simons trilogy comprised of *Lighthouse, New Moon Rising,* and *Beloved Invader?*

A. Eugenia Price.

◆

Q. What cartoon strip series was based on characters who lived in the Okefenokee Swamp?

A. Pogo.

◆

Q. What is the Southeast's largest professional nonprofit theater group?

A. The Alliance Theatre, Atlanta.

◆

Q. Rabun County high-school teacher Eliot Wigginton was the editor of what series of best-selling books?

A. *Foxfire.*

◆

Q. What Georgia-born gospel music composer wrote such classics as "Where No One Stands Alone," "Till the Storm Passes By," "Then I Met the Master," and "How Long Has It Been?"

A. Mosie Lister.

Q. St. Simons Island resident Joyce Blackburn is known for what series of children's books?

A. The Suki series.

◆

Q. Where was the United Sacred Harp Musical Association founded and based in 1904?

A. Atlanta.

◆

Q. What pioneer journal in the field of medicine was established in Augusta in 1845?

A. *Southern Medical and Surgical Journal.*

◆

Q. What book by Georgia-born Rosey Grier was published in 1973?

A. *Rosey Grier Needlepoint Book for Men.*

◆

Q. Who was the renowned painter of miniatures who died in Savannah in 1807?

A. Edward Greene Malbone.

◆

Q. In 1937 *Gone with the Wind* brought author Margaret Mitchell what coveted award?

A. The Pulitzer Prize.

◆

Q. What *Atlanta Journal* and *Constitution* newsman won a 1989 Pulitzer Prize for reporting?

A. Bill Dedman.

Q. What collection of Civil War letters from the C. C. Jones family of Liberty County won the National Book Award in 1973?

A. *The Children of Pride.*

———◆———

Q. Who was the internationally famous blind pianist and composer born a slave in 1849 on the Bethune plantation near Columbus?

A. Thomas Green Bethune, "Blind Tom."

———◆———

Q. Joel Chandler Harris spun tales of Georgia in what popular traditional black stories?

A. Uncle Remus stories.

———◆———

Q. In what town does Terry Kay, author of *To Dance with the White Dog,* live?

A. Lilburn.

———◆———

Q. Where is the Carter Library located?

A. Southwestern College, Americus.

———◆———

Q. Born in White Oak, what author is best known for the sensationalism of his novels about rural southern life?

A. Erskine Caldwll.

———◆———

Q. What was the name of Georgia's first newspaper, established in Savannah in 1763?

A. *Georgia Gazette.*

Q. The seventh book by Lewis Grizzard, a native of Moreland, Coweta County, has what title?

A. *Shoot Low Boys, They're Ridin' Shetland Ponies.*

———◆———

Q. What island hosts the annual Golden Isles Art Festival in October?

A. St. Simons Island.

———◆———

Q. On display at the Hay House in Macon is one of the "Ruth Gleaning" sculptures by what sculptor?

A. William Randolph Rogers.

———◆———

Q. What opera was presented in Atlanta at the Metropolitan Opera Company's first performance there on May 2, 1910?

A. *Lohengrin.*

———◆———

Q. Troup County has honored what well-known artist by naming an art center after him?

A. Lamar Dodd.

———◆———

Q. What composer and what lyricist wrote "Georgia on My Mind"?

A. Hoagy Carmichael and Stuart Gorrell.

———◆———

Q. What plantation served as the inspiration for Twelve Oaks in *Gone with the Wind?*

A. Lovejoy Plantation, twenty miles south of Atlanta.

Q. Who was known as "one of the world's greatest opera singers of the nineties" and kept a suite at the famous Aragon of Atlanta?

A. The "divine" Adelina Patti.

———◆———

Q. How many newspapers were there in the state by 1850?

A. Fifty-one.

———◆———

Q. In 1894, Atlanta published a new type of newspaper, a scandal sheet, by what name?

A. *The Looking Glass.*

———◆———

Q. Who was the most noted colonial Georgian potter?

A. Andrew Duché.

———◆———

Q. What Americus-born composer/guitarist wrote "Black Jazz," "White Jazz," and "Casa Loma Stomp"?

A. Harold Eugene ("Gene") Gifford.

———◆———

Q. What one-time star reporter for the *Atlanta Constitution* wrote *Cora Potts* in 1929 and *Death in the Deep South* in 1936?

A. Ward Greene.

———◆———

Q. Who was the youthful local poet who named the community of Halcyondale, located south of Sylvania in Screven County?

A. Cuyler Young.

Q. Who organized a Georgia chapter of the American Guild of Organists in 1914?

A. Edwin Arthur Kraft.

◆

Q. Who wrote *Some Go Up* and *Old Lady's Shoes,* both of which are set in the author's native Atlanta?

A. Samuel Tupper, Jr.

◆

Q. Edison Marshall became nationally famous for what type of writing?

A. Adventure stories.

◆

Q. In 1927 Marie Conway Oemler wrote what popular romance novel?

A. *Slippy McGee.*

◆

Q. Carl Brandt, who served as director of Savannah's Telfair Academy, was best known as what type of painter?

A. Muralist.

◆

Q. What noted New England artist and inventor spent time painting portraits in Darien?

A. Samuel F. B. Morse.

◆

Q. For what work is poet Robert Loveman best remembered?

A. *Rain Song.*

Q. What cartoonist created the character Mark Trail and had his comic strip collection on display at Gainesville's Green Street Station?

A. Ed Dodd.

———◆———

Q. What is the name of the oldest continuously published newspaper in the state, dating back to 1785?

A. The *Augusta Chronicle*.

———◆———

Q. Where is the home of the Columbus Symphony?

A. Three Arts Theater.

———◆———

Q. Who founded the *Columbus Enquirer* in 1828 and went on to become the president of the Republic of Texas?

A. Mirabeau Buonaparte Lamar.

———◆———

Q. The drama *Prelude to a Kiss* transferred from off-Broadway to Broadway in 1990 and won what Georgia-born playwright a Best Play award?

A. Craig Lucas.

———◆———

Q. What was the approximate building cost of Atlanta's High Museum of Art?

A. $20 million.

———◆———

Q. Where did poet Sidney Lanier compose his famous "Marshes of Glynn"?

A. Lanier Oak near Brunswick.

Q. Tina McElroy Ansa, author of the 1989 novel *Baby of the Family*, lives on what island?

A. St. Simons.

◆

Q. What childhood tragedy marked the life of Pulitzer Prize-winning poet Conrad Aiken?

A. His father, a Savannah physician, shot his wife and then himself.

◆

Q. What Atlanta artist is known in the Southeast as a portrait painter and watercolorist and has done several book illustrations including those for Celestine Sibley's classic *Christmas in Georgia?*

A. Scarlett Blanton Rickenbacker.

◆

Q. What is the name of author Joel Chandler Harris' Atlanta home?

A. Wren's Nest.

◆

Q. During the early days of the Met, what renowned opera singer made his first southern appearance as Radames in *Aïda* and as Canio in *I Pagliacci?*

A. Enrico Caruso.

◆

Q. What was the state's first black newspaper, established in Augusta in 1865?

A. *The Colored American.*

◆

Q. What Cuthbert-born jazz great introduced the concept of "big band" divided into brass, reed, and rhythm sections?

A. Fletcher Henderson.

Q. The 1991 nonfiction book *Praying for Sheetrock,* by Melissa Fay Greene of Atlanta, describes corruption in what coastal area?

A. McIntosh County.

———————◆———————

Q. One of the most valuable sources of insight into pioneer life between 1737 and 1741 may be found in the journals of what early Georgian?

A. William Stephens.

———————◆———————

Q. What Liberty County slave escaped to become a Union army nurse, later publishing her memoirs in *Reminiscences of My Life in Camp?*

A. Susie King Taylor.

———————◆———————

Q. In the pre–Revolutionary period, by what name were traveling itinerant painters known?

A. Rider artists.

———————◆———————

Q. Where was the birthplace of black musician Thomas Andrew Dorsey, composer/arranger of more than 1,000 blues and gospel songs, including "There'll Be Peace in the Valley"?

A. Villa Rica (1899).

———————◆———————

Q. What was the title of Rosalynn Carter's best-selling 1984–1985 book?

A. *First Lady from Plains.*

———————◆———————

Q. What is the name of the Dillard community center for the arts, established in 1934?

A. Hambidge Center.

Q. Where did the Uncle Remus stories first appear in print?

A. The *Atlanta Constitution*.

◆

Q. What Eatonton native won the Pulitzer Prize for Fiction in 1983?

A. Alice Walker, for *The Color Purple*.

◆

Q. The black Big Bethel Choir of Atlanta was known for what musical folk play?

A. *Heaven Bound*.

◆

Q. What Savannah-born sculptor was internationally known for his bronze animal works?

A. Edward Kemeys.

◆

Q. The adjustment of a young artist to the commercial community around him is the subject of what 1938 novel by Harry Lee?

A. *The Fox in the Cloak*.

◆

Q. What well-known black writer authored *Fire and Flint*?

A. Walter White.

◆

Q. In 1955 Savannah-born Flannery O'Connor wrote a collection of short stories by what title?

A. *A Good Man Is Hard to Find*.

Q. What is the title of the book by Caroline C. Lovell concerning the history and development of Georgia's coastal islands?

A. *The Golden Isles of Georgia.*

Q. Where is the Roddenberg Memorial Library?

A. Cairo.

Q. Gov. Zell Miller is the author of what books on his state?

A. *Great Georgians* and *They Heard Georgia Singing.*

Q. What is the official state song, selected on April 24, 1979?

A. "Georgia On My Mind."

Q. What Atlanta theater presents the Best of Broadway plays?

A. The Fox.

Q. What Decatur college administrator and Methodist minister wrote *A Treasury of Georgia Tales?*

A. Webb Garrison, in 1987.

Q. What famous fiction writer was born in Alma?

A. Harry Crews.

Q. Where is the home of the internationally acclaimed Atlanta Symphony Orchestra?

A. Robert W. Woodruff Arts Center.

———◆———

Q. Who wrote *Road to Tara*, the life of Margaret Mitchell?

A. Anne Edwards.

———◆———

Q. In what city did poet Stephen Vincent Benet begin his writing career?

A. Augusta.

———◆———

Q. What 1984 book explored the social history of the South?

A. *Southerners All*, by Dr. Nash Boney of the University of Georgia.

———◆———

Q. What was Sidney Lanier's philosophical prose work which set about to prove an inseparable relationship between the laws of verse and music?

A. *The Science of English Verse*, 1880.

———◆———

Q. What novel by Caroline Miller won the 1934 Pulitzer Prize?

A. *Lamb in His Bosom*.

———◆———

Q. What Atlanta author was a journalist for the *Atlanta Journal* and the *Atlanta Constitution* and a syndicated columnist in over 200 newspapers nationwide?

A. Lewis Grizzard.

Q. What turn-of-the-century work by Robert Cole and William Johnson became the first successful black musical comedy written for black performers?

A. *A Trip to Coontown.*

◆

Q. What Atlanta-born jazz composer has said, "We are the interpreters of Nature's Music. We find that everything on the earth contributes to its harmony?"

A. Norris Jones Sirone.

◆

Q. What non–Georgian wrote *I Am a Fugitive from a Georgia Chain Gang?*

A. Robert W. Burns.

◆

Q. What Atlanta organization was formed in 1909 to inaugurate the opening of the municipal auditorium and an annual music festival?

A. Atlanta Music Festival Association.

◆

Q. Who was the noted poet, priest, and long-time Augusta resident who penned such tributes to the Confederacy as "The Conquered Banner"?

A. Father Abram Joseph Ryan.

◆

Q. Which black singer born in Tennille in 1928 won the 1947 National Competition for Soloists Award from the Boston Pops Orchestra?

A. McHenry Rutherford Boatwright.

◆

Q. American novelist Carson McCullers was born in what Georgia city?

A. Columbus.

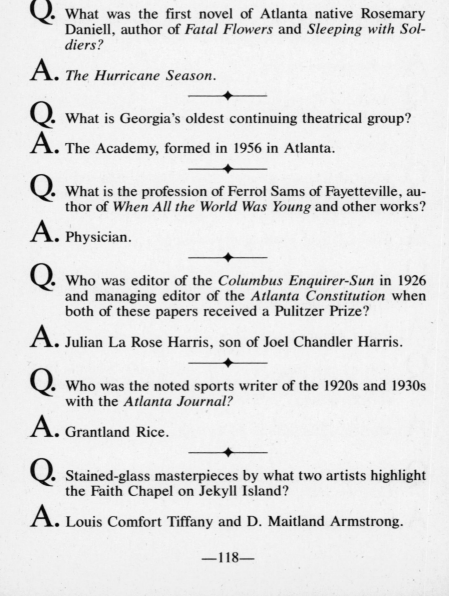

Q. What book, edited by Jane Bonner Peacock, has given us a collection of letters written by Margaret Mitchell from 1919 to 1921?

A. *Margaret Mitchell: A Dynamo Going to Waste*.

◆

Q. What was the first novel of Atlanta native Rosemary Daniell, author of *Fatal Flowers* and *Sleeping with Soldiers?*

A. *The Hurricane Season*.

◆

Q. What is Georgia's oldest continuing theatrical group?

A. The Academy, formed in 1956 in Atlanta.

◆

Q. What is the profession of Ferrol Sams of Fayetteville, author of *When All the World Was Young* and other works?

A. Physician.

◆

Q. Who was editor of the *Columbus Enquirer-Sun* in 1926 and managing editor of the *Atlanta Constitution* when both of these papers received a Pulitzer Prize?

A. Julian La Rose Harris, son of Joel Chandler Harris.

◆

Q. Who was the noted sports writer of the 1920s and 1930s with the *Atlanta Journal?*

A. Grantland Rice.

◆

Q. Stained-glass masterpieces by what two artists highlight the Faith Chapel on Jekyll Island?

A. Louis Comfort Tiffany and D. Maitland Armstrong.

Q. The best-selling novel ever written, *Gone with the Wind,* has been translated into how many languages?

A. Thirty-six.

———◆———

Q. Lowell Mason, who composed such nineteenth-century hymns as "Nearer My God to Thee," began his musical career in which Georgia city?

A. Savannah.

———◆———

Q. What Georgia town was the model for Olive Ann Burns best-selling novel *Cold Sassy Tree?*

A. Commerce.

———◆———

Q. What architect designed the High Museum of Art?

A. Richard Meier.

———◆———

Q. Who founded the *Atlanta Constitution* in 1868?

A. Colonel Carey W. Styles.

———◆———

Q. What book, written by Lucius D. Clay, is based on his experiences in military government?

A. *Decision in Germany,* 1950.

———◆———

Q. What 1932 novel by Erskine Caldwell focuses on the poverty, ignorance, and disease of the sharecropper class?

A. *Tobacco Road.*

Q. What 50-foot-high, 400-foot-circumference painting-in-the-round depicts the 1864 Battle of Atlanta?

A. Cyclorama.

◆

Q. What Atlanta-born pianist and composer received an award from BMI for over one million broadcast performances of his composition *Canadian Sunset?*

A. Eddie Heywood, Jr.

◆

Q. Bailey White, who teaches elementary school in south Georgia, reads her essays and stories on what nationally syndicated public radio program?

A. "All Things Considered."

◆

Q. What Georgian author penned the two sharply ironic novels *The Hard-boiled Virgin* in 1926 and *Dead Lovers Are Faithful Lovers* in 1928?

A. Frances Newman.

◆

Q. The tales of Elmer Ransom feature what kind of characters?

A. Animals.

◆

Q. Where is the 1918 birthplace of concert singer Carol Lovette Hawkins Brice?

A. Sedalia.

◆

Q. *Georgia Place-Names* was published in 1975 by what Macon resident?

A. Kenneth K. Krakow.

Q. Who was the New York native educator and clergyman who wrote the *Gazetteer of the State of Georgia* in the 1820s and 1830s?

A. Adiel Sherwood.

———◆———

Q. Who is the conductor of the Atlanta Symphony?

A. Yoel Levi.

———◆———

Q. What 1952 book described the antebellum mansions and plantations of Georgia?

A. *White Columns in Georgia* by Medora Field Perkerson of Atlanta.

———◆———

Q. Who was the well-known nineteenth-century author who wrote the juvenile books *Young Marooners* in 1852 and *Marooners' Island* in 1862?

A. F. R. Goulding.

———◆———

Q. What Georgia city is the setting for Willie Snow Ethridge's memoirs, *As I Live and Breathe?*

A. Macon.

———◆———

Q. The rural development of a cappella singing by reading shaped-note music led to the participants being called by what name?

A. Fasola singers.

———◆———

Q. What Atlanta-born poet, novelist, film-maker, and critic was known for such works as *The Strength of the Fields*, 1979; *Scion*, 1980; and *Deliverance: A Screenplay*, 1981?

A. James Dickey.

Q. What noted Civil War scholar wrote of "Jane Reb" in his 1975 book *Confederate Women?*

A. Dr. Bell Irvin Wiley of Emory University.

◆

Q. Where can you visit Georgia's first privately endowed public library?

A. Washington.

◆

Q. For euphony, Stephen Foster deliberately misspelled the name of what river in one of his most popular songs?

A. Suwanee ("Old Folks at Home" or "Way Down Upon the Swanee River").

◆

Q. Who authored a 1982 collection of black folk tales from rural Georgia entitled *Hush, Child, Can't You Hear the Music?*

A. Rose Thompson.

◆

Q. Dalton's Creative Arts Guild for performing and visual arts is housed in what type of building?

A. The old firehouse.

◆

Q. Who painted the murals at the U. S. Federal Building and Post Office in Macon, depicting the history of the area?

A. George Beattie.

◆

Q. What newspaper woman penned the 1930 novel *Secret Fathers?*

A. Mildred Seydell.

Q. What folk opera did Hall Johnson, a choir director from Athens, compose?

A. *Run, Little Chillun.*

Q. Who wrote *History of Savannah and South Georgia* in 1913?

A. William Harden.

Q. Where is the Springer Opera House?

A. Columbus.

Q. Who received national acclaim for *The Tragedy of Lynching,* a work dealing with interracial relations?

A. Arthur Raper.

Q. What Atlanta writer depicted the social life of her city in *Peachtree Road?*

A. Anne Rivers Siddons.

Q. Who was awarded the 1896 *Chicago Record* prize for his work *Sons and Fathers?*

A. Harry Stillwell Edwards.

Q. What Georgia-born writer produced *Member of the Wedding?*

A. Carson McCullers.

Q. The Douglas County community of Bill Arp was named for the pen name of which southern humorist/newspaper editor?

A. Charles Henry Smith.

◆

Q. What Atlanta-born composer was the only non–Ellington alumnus to perform for the Duke Ellington Society and arrange the music for Ellington's seventy-fourth birthday party?

A. Columbus Calvin ("Duke") Pearson, Jr.

◆

Q. Georgia writer Berry Fleming is best known for what 1935 novel with a southern setting?

A. *Siesta.*

◆

Q. Who edited the *Atlanta Constitution* from 1879 until his death and was known as the voice of the New South?

A. Henry Woodfin Grady (1850–1889).

◆

Q. Nineteenth-century painter William Posey Silva is best known for what subject matter?

A. Landscapes.

◆

Q. What play by Lula Vollmer served as a vivid dramatization of southern mountaineer life?

A. *Sun Up,* 1924.

◆

Q. Where is the Uncle Remus Museum and Statue honoring the works of Joel Chandler Harris?

A. Eatonton.

Q. What Georgia biographer is known for her works on Martha Berry, James Oglethorpe, Theodore Roosevelt, John Adams, and George Wythe?

A. Joyce Blackburn.

◆

Q. What was the first book by Corra Harris which brought her to national attention in 1910?

A. *A Circuit Rider's Wife*.

◆

Q. What serial written and published by Baldwin Longstreet in the *Augusta Sentinel* humorously depicted the vigorous lifestyles of Georgians in the 1830s?

A. *Georgia Scenes*.

◆

Q. Who authored the well-known state historical book *A Short History of Georgia?*

A. Merton Coulter.

◆

Q. Where did Rembrandt and Raphael Peale establish a shop in 1804 to produce portraits, silhouettes, and miniatures?

A. Savannah.

◆

Q. Who wrote the 1938 novel *Mingled Yarn,* dealing with the problems of a young mill town couple?

A. Willie Snow Ethridge.

◆

Q. Who was the first American woman to own and edit a newspaper?

A. Sarah Porter Hillhouse, *The Washington Gazette*.

Q. The *Story of France,* 1898, and *Napoleon,* 1903, are works of what turn-of-the-century Georgian writer?

A. Thomas E. Watson.

Q. What was the name of the hymnal compiled by John Wesley in Savannah which became the first Methodist hymnal ever published?

A. *A Collection of Psalms and Hymns.*

Q. What book by Atlanta journalist Celestine Sibley depicts southern life?

A. *For All Seasons.*

Q. Peter Marshall, the subject of the best seller *A Man Called Peter,* graduated from what Georgia institution in 1931?

A. Columbia Theological Seminary, Decatur.

Q. Thomas and Lucy Carnegie built their magnificent home Dungeness on what island?

A. Cumberland Island.

Q. What Confederate army general was elected to the Georgia senate, served as governor, and published the book *Reminiscences of the Civil War?*

A. John Brown Gordon (1832–1904).

Q. The famous "unfinished portrait" of Franklin D. Roosevelt hangs in what museum?

A. Franklin D. Roosevelt Museum at Warm Springs.

Q. Where in Albany can a variety of comedies, musicals, dramas, and children's theater productions be viewed?

A. Little Theatre.

———◆———

Q. The Macon City Auditorium houses what large musical instrument?

A. Pipe organ.

———◆———

Q. Which Georgia newspaper editor won a 1959 Pulitzer Prize for editorial writing?

A. Ralph McGill, *Atlanta Constitution*.

———◆———

Q. What 1906 book published by Augustus Longstreet Hull dealt with the settlement and development of Athens?

A. *Annals of Athens, Georgia, 1801–1901*.

———◆———

Q. Who was the poet, noted for his tortuous idioms and overornamentation, who published *The Lost Pleiad and Other Poems* in 1842?

A. Thomas Holley Chivers.

———◆———

Q. Who won the 1930 annual award of the Poetry Society of America for his work *Strange Splendor?*

A. Ernest Hartsock.

———◆———

Q. What Atlanta writer was best known for her 1944 *Strange Fruit?*

A. Lillian Smith.

Q. What 1935 work by Walter Mills analyzes the propaganda which aroused America to participate in World War I?

A. *Road to War.*

———◆———

Q. In 1900 what world-renowned pianist, who later became Poland's president, gave a recital at the Grand Theater?

A. Ignace Jan Paderewski.

———◆———

Q. Though often a writer of novels with a foreign setting, Isa Glenn wrote what book in 1930 set in Georgia?

A. *A Short History of Julia.*

———◆———

Q. In what book did former president Jimmy Carter depict his political career in Georgia?

A. *The Turning Point.*

———◆———

Q. The classic Renaissance-style capitol building in Atlanta was designed by what architectural firm?

A. Edbrooke and Burnham of Chicago.

———◆———

Q. A widely publicized 1913 murder case led to what ballad?

A. "The Death of Mary Phagen."

———◆———

Q. Who was the most popular Georgian poet of the 1890s?

A. Frank L. Stanton.

SPORTS & LEISURE

CHAPTER FOUR

Q. What team were the Atlanta Braves playing when Hank Aaron broke Babe Ruth's home run record?

A. Los Angeles Dodgers, April 8, 1974.

◆

Q. What city hosts the Georgia State Fair each October?

A. Macon, since 1851.

◆

Q. What was the name of the nine-hole golf course built for the millionaire members of the Jekyll Island Club?

A. Oceanside Nine.

◆

Q. What Georgia Bulldog received the Heisman Trophy in 1982?

A. Herschel Walker.

◆

Q. What Bainbridge-born top boxing contender lost only 15 of 127 professional fights?

A. William Lawrence ("Young") Stribling II.

Q. The one tie in Georgia Tech's 11–0–1 1990–1991 football season record was with what team?

A. North Carolina (13–13).

◆

Q. Which family owned Jekyll Island prior to the millionaires?

A. The du Bignon family.

◆

Q. What fullback for the Cleveland Browns was born on St. Simons Island and led the National Football League in rushing for eight of his nine years of play?

A. Jim Brown.

◆

Q. In what year was the National Baseball League established, of which the Braves are charter members?

A. 1876.

◆

Q. What Walthourville native became the only cyclist to hold the national and world titles simultaneously and was known as the Dixie Worldwind?

A. Bobby Walthour, Sr.

◆

Q. Fitzgerald, which originated as a Union soldiers' colony, is now home for what museum?

A. The Blue Gray Museum.

◆

Q. The Lookout Mountain Flight Park is the site of what exciting sport?

A. Hang gliding.

Q. Who purchased the Atlanta Braves in 1976?

A. R. E. ("Ted") Turner.

———◆———

Q. Who is known as the Sports Doc, the founder and director of the Hughston Sports Medicine Hospital and Campus in Columbus?

A. Jack Hughston.

———◆———

Q. What 1936 gold medalist in the 110-meter hurdles and track coach at Georgia died in Athens on April 9, 1991?

A. Forrest ("Spec") Towns.

———◆———

Q. What part of the Flint River is said to have destroyed more canoes than any other single rapid in the Southeast?

A. Yellow Jacket Shoals.

———◆———

Q. What is the name of the collection of authentic log cabins on display at Fort Gaines?

A. Frontier Village.

———◆———

Q. What was the score of the 1987 Liberty Bowl game in Memphis?

A. Georgia 20, Arkansas 17.

———◆———

Q. What governor signed into law the bill to create the Georgia Sports Hall of Fame?

A. Governor George Busbee, 1978.

Q. On May 7, 1985, what favorite New York Knicks player became assistant coach with the Atlanta Hawks?

A. Willis Reed.

＊

Q. Sam Jones ("Sambo") Elliott, McDonough native, was elected to what Hall of Fame in 1957?

A. The National Softball Hall of Fame.

＊

Q. The Falcon Training Complex, year-round home of the Falcons, is in what community?

A. Suwannee.

＊

Q. What Georgian won the 1938 black national golf championship?

A. Howard Wheeler.

＊

Q. Which lake has been called the Houseboat Capital of the World?

A. Lanier Lake.

＊

Q. Who was the Georgian who won the national clay courts tennis championship in 1930, 1934, and 1935?

A. Bryan ("Bitsy") Grant.

＊

Q. What University of Georgia football player received the South's first Heisman Trophy in 1942?

A. Frank Sinkwich.

Q. What Atlanta-born golfer was the women pro tour's leading money winner from 1953 to 1960?

A. Louise Suggs.

━━━━◆━━━━

Q. In what two Georgia cities will the 1996 Olympic Games be played?

A. Atlanta and Savannah.

━━━━◆━━━━

Q. What annual ethnic celebration takes place at Old Fort Jackson the first Saturday in May?

A. The Scottish Games.

━━━━◆━━━━

Q. What Atlanta Brave pitched a no-hitter over San Diego, August 5, 1973?

A. Phil Niekro.

━━━━◆━━━━

Q. Who was Best Athlete at Lanier High 1943–1945 and earned eleven letters at Georgia Tech before beginning an outstanding coaching career?

A. Jim Nolan.

━━━━◆━━━━

Q. In 1927, who led the New York Giants to the world championship after being All-Southern fullback for Georgia Tech three straight years, 1923–1925?

A. Doug Wycoff.

━━━━◆━━━━

Q. Beginning the first Saturday in November and ending the last Saturday in March, Thomson participants dress in scarlet and black for what sporting event?

A. The Belle Meade Fox Hunt.

Q. Born in Atlanta in 1938, Mack Jones played outfield during a ten-year period for the Milwaukee Braves, Atlanta Braves, Cincinnati Reds, and Montreal Expos and was known by what nickname?

A. The Knife.

◆

Q. What was the favorite sport of the Cherokee Indians of Georgia?

A. Stick ball, similar to lacrosse.

◆

Q. Who is the Rome-born Atlanta Hawk whose father was head basketball coach at the Georgia School for the Deaf?

A. Mike Glenn.

◆

Q. Augusta is the home of what internationally famous golfing event?

A. The Masters Golf Tournament.

◆

Q. Claxton and Wigham are noted for what type of yearly roundups?

A. Rattlesnake.

◆

Q. Before moving to Atlanta, the Braves were associated with what two cities?

A. Boston and Milwaukee.

◆

Q. What Carrollton native was known as the Adolph Rupp of Georgia high school basketball?

A. Eric P. Staples.

Q. Beau Jack, shoeshine boy at Augusta National, later held what famous world championship title?

A. World lightweight boxing champion.

◆

Q. What Georgia Tech coach and National Hall of Famer was the first to coach six major bowl winners in consecutive years and coached the All-Stars in the Miami North–South Shrine game (1950–1957)?

A. Robert Lee ("Bobby") Dodd.

◆

Q. The Washington–Wilkes Historical Museum in Washington is noted for what type of Civil War memorabilia?

A. Confederate gun collection.

◆

Q. What forward of the Atlanta Hawks made the All-NBA second team in 1991?

A. Dominique Wilkins.

◆

Q. In what city is the Chieftains Museum?

A. Rome.

◆

Q. Known as a great relief pitcher, what Buckhead-born player won fame in the 1940s with the Brooklyn Dodgers?

A. Hugh Casey.

◆

Q. Len Hauss of Washington Redskins fame is from what community?

A. Jesup.

Q. Where was the birthplace of Jackie Robinson, the first black man to play major league ball?

A. Cairo.

◆

Q. Where would you find one of the finest ships-in-a-bottle collections in the world?

A. Ships of the Sea, a maritime museum in Savannah.

◆

Q. What former University of Georgia football coach was given the title Great White Football Father?

A. Pop Warner.

◆

Q. As of 1994, how many times have the Atlanta Falcons made it to the Super Bowl?

A. Zero.

◆

Q. Who was the Macon-born favorite L.A. Dodger, known as Mr. Clutch?

A. Ronald Ray Fairly.

◆

Q. What Toccoa High athlete gained fame by winning the gold medal in the 1956 Olympics, making him the "World's Strongest Man"?

A. Paul Anderson.

◆

Q. What Georgia Tech coach was the first to put his team in all the major bowls, Rose (1928), Orange (1939 and 1944), Cotton (1942), and Sugar (1943)?

A. W. A. Alexander.

Q. What professional baseball player was nicknamed the Georgia Peach?

A. Tyrus Raymond ("Ty") Cobb.

Q. Where is the world's largest manmade sand beach?

A. Callaway Gardens.

Q. What annual crafts fair has its home in Chatsworth?

A. Fort Mountain Village Crafts Fair.

Q. What All-American and All-Southeastern Conference guard at Georgia Tech, 1951, later became affiliated with the New York Giants?

A. Ray Beck.

Q. What Atlanta golfer realized her goal of winning the USGA's national women's amateur golf championship in 1951?

A. Dorothy ("Dot") Kirby.

Q. What collegiate football bowl takes place in Atlanta?

A. Peach Bowl.

Q. Who became the first athlete to win an Olympic gold medal while representing a southern school?

A. Edward B. Hamm, Georgia Tech track (1926–30).

Q. What fall festival is held in Camilla?

A. The Corn Festival.

◆

Q. What Buchanan farmer took the 1954 Crackers to a win of the Southern Association pennant, all-star games, playoffs, and Dixie series?

A. John Whitlow Wyatt.

◆

Q. Who was Georgia's first selection for the National Football Hall of Fame?

A. Robert ("Bob") McWhorter.

◆

Q. On November 3, 1990, number-one ranked Virginia lost a home football game to what school, 41–38?

A. Georgia Tech.

◆

Q. Columbus Drive Field, Cobb County, is the home of what aristocratic sport?

A. Polo.

◆

Q. What Atlanta Hawk was the NBA scoring leader in 1986 with 2,366 points, a 30.3 average?

A. Dominique Wilkins.

◆

Q. What Atlanta race car driver became NASCAR's first king of the oval tracks by winning 40 races in fewer than 250 starts through 1956?

A. Tim Flock.

Q. As of 1994, what was Georgia's all-time bowl record?

A. 15–13–3.

◆

Q. Luke ("Old Aches and Pains") Appling, minor league hitting instructor for the Atlanta Braves since retiring from the Chicago White Sox in 1950, died January 3, 1991, in what Georgia town?

A. Cumming.

◆

Q. What World Wrestling Federation champ nicknamed Mr. Wonderful now resides in Atlanta?

A. Paul Orndorff.

◆

Q. Wyomia Tyus, track star who began training at Fairmount High in Griffin, brought home the gold, winning the 100-yard dash in what Olympics?

A. 1964 Olympics, Tokyo.

◆

Q. The Atlanta International Raceway hosts what two Grand National stock car races?

A. The *Atlanta Journal* 500 and the Coca-Cola 500.

◆

Q. Pine Mountain, between Warm Springs and Callaway, offers a swimming pool in what unforgettable shape?

A. The Liberty Bell.

◆

Q. Besides Braves baseball and Falcon football, what other two sporting events are held annually at the Atlanta–Fulton County Stadium?

A. Peach Bowl and Motocross race.

Q. Who coached Gainesville to a state basketball title in 1949?

A. Drane Watson.

◆

Q. The U.S. Orienteering Federation has its headquarters in what Georgia town?

A. Forest Park.

◆

Q. What Georgia-born sportsman of the early 1930s, known as the Emperor of Golf, won the American Amateur, the American Open, the British Amateur, and the British Open, all within one year?

A. Robert Tyre ("Bobby") Jones, Jr.

◆

Q. In what year did the Braves move to Atlanta?

A. 1966.

◆

Q. Who produced more big-league ball players than any other coach and is still known as Father of Oglethorpe University Athletics?

A. Frank B. Anderson, Sr.

◆

Q. What two Atlanta Falcons made the All-Pro first team in 1991?

A. Wide receiver Andre Rison and cornerback Deion Sanders.

◆

Q. The Gold Museum is located in which town?

A. Dahlonega.

Q. George M. Phillips, who officiated in Southern and Southeastern conferences from 1929 to 1945, was known by what nickname?

A. Pup.

———◆———

Q. The Sur-Way Tomboys, who won the women's major slow pitch championship in 1981 and 1986, are from what town?

A. Tifton.

———◆———

Q. John W. Heisman coached at Georgia Tech during what time period?

A. 1904–1919.

———◆———

Q. Where in Columbus are the hulls of the ironclad *Jackson* and the gunboat *Chattahoochee* on display?

A. The Confederate Naval Museum.

———◆———

Q. John ("Whack") Hyder, coach of Georgia Tech basketball for over two decades and professional baseball player for three years, is from what Georgia community?

A. Lula.

———◆———

Q. What Buena Vista-born ball player gained the distinction of being the greatest home run hitter in the Negro Baseball League?

A. Josh Gibson.

———◆———

Q. What city hosts the Ogeechee River Raft Race?
A. Statesboro.

Q. Atlanta athlete John Carson starred nine years as wide receiver for what NFL team?

A. Washington Redskins.

——◆——

Q. What Athens native became the winningest active college tennis coach in America through 1979?

A. Dan Magill.

——◆——

Q. Where was the birthplace of Rosey Grier, pro football player with the New York Giants?

A. Cuthbert.

——◆——

Q. Georgia Tech coach Bill Fincher fashioned his own shoulder pads from what item?

A. A horse collar.

——◆——

Q. In what three years did Lucy Wener of the University of Georgia win the uneven bars individual championship in gymnastics?

A. 1986, 1987, and 1989.

——◆——

Q. In what city is the Georgia Sports Hall of Fame?

A. Atlanta.

——◆——

Q. What Atlanta Hawk was a member of the gold-medal United States Olympic basketball team in 1984?

A. Jon Koncak.

Q. What Macon native played for the Baltimore Colts from 1957 to 1967?

A. Jim Parker.

———◆———

Q. What Columbus High athlete went on to captain the 1940 Bulldogs?

A. James Skipworth, Jr.

———◆———

Q. What annual golfing event is held at Perry?

A. The Houston Lake Pro-Am Classic.

———◆———

Q. Cordele is host to what July event?

A. Watermelon Festival.

———◆———

Q. In what year was Georgia-born Ty Cobb elected to the National Baseball Hall of Fame?

A. 1936.

———◆———

Q. In what year did Tim Witherspoon defeat Tony Tubbs in a World Heavyweight Championship fight in Atlanta?

A. 1986.

———◆———

Q. What Commerce-born pitcher became the American League's Most Valuable Player in 1943?

A. Spurgeon ("Spud") Chandler.

Q. Barnett native Jim Bagby, Sr., who won thirty-one games in 1920 to help lead Cleveland to its first American League pennant, was known by what nickname?

A. Sarge.

———◆———

Q. What is the name of the authentic split sternwheel excursion riverboat based in Columbus?

A. *Jubilee.*

———◆———

Q. Vince Dooley is the seven-time winner of what outstanding honor?

A. SEC Coach of the Year (1964, '66, '68, '76, '78, '80, '81).

———◆———

Q. What Atlanta Archer High student went on to Tennessee State and took the world of track by storm, winning the gold in the 1964 Olympics for the 200-meter dash?

A. Edith McGuire Duvall.

———◆———

Q. Where did the Georgia Tech football team rank in the UPI polls for the 1990–91 season?

A. First.

———◆———

Q. Cochran is host to what May festival?

A. Gum Swamp Festival.

———◆———

Q. What Decatur High football coach won forty-two games, losing only one conference game, from 1930 to 1933?

A. H. D. ("Dickie") Butler.

Q. What coveted trophy was claimed by the Bulldogs in 1985 for being the SEC school with the most successful overall men's sports program?

A. Bernie Moore trophy.

------◆------

Q. What city hosts the annual Crowe Springs Craftsmen's Fair in October?

A. Cartersville.

------◆------

Q. As a pioneer Georgia high school coach from 1912 to 1934, who organized the first basketball teams at Mineral Bluff, Omega, Pineview, Vienna, and Norman Institute?

A. Joe H. Jenkins.

------◆------

Q. Where is the National Infantry Museum located, tracing the history of the infantry from the French and Indian War to the present?

A. Fort Benning.

------◆------

Q. What Georgia Bulldog was known as America's fastest man in water in the 1950s, smashing records in the 1956 Melbourne Olympics?

A. Logan Reid Patterson.

------◆------

Q. Which University of Georgia women's team won national championships in 1987 and 1989?

A. Gymnastics.

------◆------

Q. What two teams played the first game in the Atlanta–Fulton County Stadium on April 9, 1965?

A. The Milwaukee Braves defeated the Detroit Tigers, 6–3.

Q. Who were the two wealthiest owners of "millionaire cottages" on Jekyll Island?

A. John D. Rockefeller and J. P. Morgan.

◆

Q. What former Atlanta Brave stands second to Henry Aaron in most games played by a Brave in Atlanta?

A. Mike Lum.

◆

Q. In 1991, Georgia Tech beat Nebraska by what score in the Florida Citrus Bowl?

A. 45–21.

◆

Q. Theo ("Tiger") Flowers, known as the Georgia Deacon, held what world championship title in 1926?

A. World middleweight boxing champion.

◆

Q. What city hosts the bi-annual Crackerland Country Fair?

A. Howard.

◆

Q. What Georgia coach is credited with introducing zone defense to the South?

A. H. J. Stegeman.

◆

Q. What educator, Baptist minister, and coach, who played basketball, baseball, football, and starred in track at Mercer University, was known as the greatest athlete in the South from 1921 to 1925?

A. B. L. ("Crook") Smith.

Q. Who served seventeen years as the first athletic director of Atlanta schools, beginning in 1947, and was later to become the first executive director of the Atlanta–Fulton County Stadium?

A. Sidney Scarborough.

———◆———

Q. What type of racehorse training facilities are located in Hawkinsville?

A. Harness Training Tracks.

———◆———

Q. Called the Miracle Man, what Augusta native managed the Boston Braves from last place to a National League pennant and a World Series sweep?

A. George Tweedy Stallings.

———◆———

Q. In what year did Georgia beat Michigan State 34–27 in the Gator Bowl?

A. 1989.

———◆———

Q. What Gainesville High and Georgia athlete pitched for the 1959 Atlanta Crackers?

A. Jack Roberts.

———◆———

Q. Where can you participate in the July Appalachian Wagon Train?

A. Chatsworth.

———◆———

Q. Who was known for introducing numerous sportswriting innovations during his 1934–1976 career at the *Atlanta Constitution?*

A. Charles N. Roberts.

Q. In what year did John ("Stumpy") Thomason, one of Atlanta Tech High's best halfbacks, lead Georgia Tech to a Rose Bowl championship?

A. 1928.

◆

Q. Who is said to be the most successful minor-league operator of all time and was president and owner of the Atlanta Crackers from 1933 to 1959?

A. Earl Mann.

◆

Q. What is the name of the skiing resort located in Rabun County that offers natural and manmade snow?

A. Sky Valley.

◆

Q. Macon native Johnny Lee ("Blue Moon") Odom pitched for what major-league clubs during his thirteen-year playing career?

A. Kansas City A's, Oakland A's, Cleveland Indians, Chicago White Sox, and Atlanta Braves.

◆

Q. What Buena Vista resident won the 1992 U.S. National Rifle Association International Trap Shooting championship?

A. Bret Erickson.

◆

Q. What raceway is the home to the Canadian–American Challenge Cup?

A. Road Atlanta.

◆

Q. Known as major league's Mr. Shortstop, what man who had his beginnings at Atlanta Tech High, played in four world series, five major-league all-star games, and managed the St. Louis Browns, Cardinals, and Chicago White Sox?

A. Martin ("Marty") Marion.

Q. Where is the Fall Music Festival and Fiddlers Convention held?

A. Hiawassee, Towns County.

◆

Q. For what professional football team did William Thomas Stanfill play, after fine careers in Cairo and at the University of Georgia?

A. Miami Dolphins, 1969–1976.

◆

Q. From Chamblee to Tokyo and Mexico City in the 1964 and 1968 Olympics, what gold-medal track star became head track coach in 1975 at the U.S. Military Academy?

A. Mel Pender.

◆

Q. Cedartown-born Philips Brooks Douglas, who began his baseball career pitching for Rome and Macon, was best known by what nickname?

A. Shufflin' Phil.

◆

Q. Which Georgia Bulldog signed with the 1985 Falcons as a free agent?

A. Wayne Radloff.

◆

Q. What city houses one of the largest indoor horse arenas in the Southeast?

A. Unadilla.

◆

Q. Where is the home court of the University of Georgia Bulldogs?

A. Georgia Coliseum.

Q. What Summerville native became pro baseball's greatest fielding shortstop in the 1930s?

A. Nolen Richardson.

Q. What former Rome manager and major-league ball player was known for having the smallest feet in the majors?

A. Myril Oliver Hoag.

Q. What city is nicknamed Golf Capital of the United States?

A. Augusta.

Q. Where is the birthplace of John Milner, who played outfield and first base for eleven years with the New York Mets, Pittsburgh Pirates, and Montreal Expos?

A. Atlanta.

Q. What is the world-renowned resort on Sea Island?

A. The Cloister.

Q. In 1983 Leonidas S. Epps retired after a thirty-four-year coaching career at what college?

A. Clark College, Atlanta.

Q. What city is host to the annual Long County Wildlife Festival in October?

A. Ludowici.

Q. What was the score of the 1991 World Series?

A. Minnesota 4, Atlanta 3.

◆

Q. What All-Star three-year halfback and two-year basketball standout went on to be inducted into the Georgia Tech Hall of Fame as halfback in 1947?

A. George Mathews.

◆

Q. What collection, one of the largest of its type in the world, is found at the Chickamauga National Military Park?

A. Fuller Gun Collection.

◆

Q. What Atlanta native served as commissioner of the SEC officials from 1947 through the 1970s?

A. George Gardner.

◆

Q. Who was the 1942 Decatur High Best All-Around Athlete who later guided the Arkansas Razorbacks to top honors in football?

A. Frank Broyles.

◆

Q. What nautical ceremony is held each May in Darien?

A. The Blessing of the Fleet.

◆

Q. What Falcon holds the record for the most touchdowns by rushing in a single season?

A. Gerald Riggs, 1985.

Q. Golden Park is the home of which baseball team?

A. Columbus Astros.

———————◆———————

Q. What Villa Rica-born outfielder with the New York Yankees, Chicago White Sox, Detroit Tigers, and the Brooklyn Dodgers was brother of batting star Harry Walker, son of Ewart Walker, and nephew of Ernie Walker, all major leaguers?

A. Frederick E. ("Dixie") Walker.

———————◆———————

Q. Which community hosts the Sunbelt Expo?

A. Moultrie.

———————◆———————

Q. The 1991 men's super slow pitch national champion team Sunbelt/Worth are from what town?

A. Centerville.

———————◆———————

Q. What was Georgia's football season record in 1980?

A. 12–0–0.

———————◆———————

Q. For twenty-four seasons, what man led the Bulldog golfers to be among the nation's best?

A. Howell Hollis.

———————◆———————

Q. What football player began at Georgia Tech in 1917 and became known as the second-best Indian player in history?

A. Indian Joe (Joseph Napoleon Guyon), second only to Jim Thorpe.

Q. Who was the leading Lanier High athlete who played football center for Georgia and later coached at the university?

A. Quinton Lumpkin.

———◆———

Q. In what town were the first movie magazines of the Southeast displayed?

A. Montgomery.

———◆———

Q. In what two consecutive seasons did Stan Kasten of the Atlanta Hawks win the NBA Executive of the Year award?

A. 1985–86 and 1986–87.

———◆———

Q. Who lead the National League in batting average and hits in 1991?

A. Atlanta Braves Terry Pendleton.

———◆———

Q. Which two weekends of the year is the Country Fair at Praters Mill, near Tunnel Hill, held?

A. Mother's Day and Columbus Day weekends.

———◆———

Q. During his eleven seasons with Atlanta, what Falcon won every football award and was very active in the Georgia Special Olympics and the founding of charity golf tournaments for the disadvantaged?

A. Tommy Nobis.

———◆———

Q. Demorest native John Mize played first base, hitting .313 and slugging 2,000 hits, for what three major-league teams?

A. St. Louis Cardinals, New York Giants, and New York Yankees.

Q. In 1905 the Detroit Tigers purchased Ty Cobb from Augusta of the South Atlantic league for what amount?

A. $500.

———◆———

Q. Multimillionaire J. P. Morgan had what type of sports facility built indoors on Jekyll Island?

A. Tennis court.

———◆———

Q. Who is credited with hitting the longest home run at the Atlanta–Fulton County Stadium?

A. Willie Smith of the Chicago Cubs, 1969.

———◆———

Q. What baseball player, discovered by Grantland Rice in Marietta, became mayor of Roswell and one of the Dodgers best-known scouts?

A. George Napoleon Rucker.

———◆———

Q. What Braves star won the 1982 and 1983 Most Valuable Player awards?

A. Dale Murphy.

———◆———

Q. The nation's only manufacturer of golf-ball molds is in what community?

A. Perry.

———◆———

Q. What cutting horse competition is the largest equestrian event of its kind east of the Mississippi?

A. Augusta Futurity.

Q. What museum is located in the keeper's cottage of the St. Simons lighthouse?

A. Museum of Coastal History.

◆

Q. What Carrollton native had great success coaching track for forty-two years and produced two Olympic winners, Spec Towns and Bobby Packard?

A. Weems Baskin.

◆

Q. Who was the witty and popular sports columnist-analyst for the *Atlanta Journal?*

A. Harry Mehre.

◆

Q. Helen is noted for what annual aeronautical event?

A. Hot Air Balloon Festival.

◆

Q. What nineteen-year-old Georgia Bulldog, along with teammate Frankie Sinkwich, was a star on the team that won against UCLA, 9–0, in the 1942 Rose Bowl?

A. Charley Trippi.

◆

Q. For how long did Young Stribling hold the world light heavyweight title after a bout in Columbus on October 4, 1923?

A. Three hours, until the referee could escape a mob and reverse his decision.

◆

Q. Why did Ty Cobb refuse to room with Babe Ruth during an exhibition tour?

A. Because of rumors that Ruth had a black heritage.

Q. Who was the youngest player to take part in a minor-league game?

A. Joe Relford, a twelve-year-old black batboy for the Fitzgerald Club in the Georgia State League on July 19, 1952.

———◆———

Q. Gainesville High produced what sportsman who won the 1973 Masters Tournament and became the first Georgia golfer to earn over $100,000 on the pro tour in one season?

A. Tommy Aaron.

———◆———

Q. What was the score of the 1992 World Series?

A. Toronto 4, Atlanta 2.

———◆———

Q. Where is the Military Museum that features displays from the Civil War to present?

A. Hinesville.

———◆———

Q. What was the nickname of 1925 Atlanta-born Harry Simpson, who played outfield for the Cleveland Indians, Kansas City Athletics, and the New York Yankees?

A. Suitcase.

———◆———

Q. What Atlanta-born runner took the 1932 Olympics silver medal in the 100 meters behind teammate Jesse Owens?

A. Ralph Metcalfe.

———◆———

Q. What Atlanta-born athlete pitched one of the New York Giants' two victories in the 1951 World Series against the Yankees?

A. James Tolbert ("Jim") Hearn.

Q. What is the name of the fieldhouse at Georgia College, Milledgeville?

A. Georgia Military Gym.

◆

Q. What Fitzgerald High School athlete was featured in Ripley's "Believe It or Not" after scoring ten touchdowns in one game?

A. Wright Bazemore.

◆

Q. Known as the Bird Dog Capital of the World, what town is the site of the annual Georgia Field Trials?

A. Waynesboro.

◆

Q. What coach became famous for producing such punters as Zeke Bratkowski, Johnny Rauch, and Cliff Kimsey, as well as coaching Georgia kickers in the 1970s?

A. Bill Hartman, Jr.

◆

Q. Having played for Brooklyn, Cleveland, and Pittsburgh from 1911 to 1927, what Mansfield-born pro baseball player was known for having the greatest pickoff move in baseball history?

A. Sherrod ("Sherry") Smith.

◆

Q. What White County-born, Georgia Hall of Famer won the 1945 Kentucky Derby with the first racehorse he ever owned?

A. Fred W. Hooper; horse: Hoop, Jr.

◆

Q. What city hosts the annual PGA Southern Open Golf Tournament?

A. Columbus.

Q. What quarterback led the Bulldogs in 1946 and 1948 to SEC titles and went on to coach Oakland to the 1967 Super Bowl?

A. Johnny Rauch.

---◆---

Q. As of 1992, the world's largest largemouth bass at twenty-two pounds, four ounces, was caught in 1932 in what Georgia lake?

A. Montgomery.

---◆---

Q. Where is the home court of the Atlanta Hawks?

A. The Omni Coliseum.

---◆---

Q. What ball player started his career in Valdosta in 1947 and went on to play in the 1955 Brooklyn and 1960 Pittsburgh World Series?

A. Donald Albert ("Tiger") Hoak.

---◆---

Q. What Bremen-born Yankee outfielder was known as Babe Ruth's leg?

A. Samuel Dewey Byrd.

---◆---

Q. Griffin schoolteacher Julia Elliott suggested the nickname for what Georgia team?

A. Falcons.

---◆---

Q. In what year did the AP and UPI choose Georgia as the National College Football Champions?

A. 1980.

Q. What tennis titleholder received the Distinguished Citizen of Newton County award for teaching tennis to Covington youngsters?

A. Mary Louise Fowler.

———◆———

Q. What Thomaston-born ball player pitched only one complete major-league game, a no-hitter?

A. Alva Lee ("Bobo") Holloman, for the St. Louis Browns, 1953.

———◆———

Q. What is the seating capacity of Sanford Stadium?

A. 82,000, the fifth-largest collegiate stadium.

———◆———

Q. What Decatur player was both a Los Angeles All-Pro linebacker and a Chicago Bear?

A. Larry Morris.

———◆———

Q. What Macon-born baseball manager is credited with developing stars Pete Rose, Tommy Helms, Lee May, and Tony Perez?

A. David Bristol.

———◆———

Q. In what year was Hope Spivey of the University of Georgia the floor-exercise and all-around individual champion in gymnastics?

A. 1991.

———◆———

Q. Where is the birthplace of Lil People and Cabbage Patch Kids?

A. Babyland General Hospital, Cleveland.

Q. What former University of Georgia football player became the 1958 NFL Rookie of the Year while playing for Pittsburgh?

A. Jimmy Orr.

Q. Track coach Jimmy Carnes, president of Athletics Congress USA, is a native of what Georgia community?

A. Eatonton.

Q. Who coached the Atlanta Falcons from 1974 to 1976?

A. Marion Campbell.

Q. Fayette County's Cecil Travis was a member of what pro baseball team?

A. Washington Senators.

Q. What Glynn County native won thirty national and international competitions for trap and skeet shooting?

A. Fred Misseldine.

Q. Who holds the all-time personal fouls record for the Atlanta Hawks?

A. Bill Bridges, 2,575 fouls.

Q. Athens High graduate Fran Tarkenton played for what two NFL teams?

A. Minnesota Vikings and New York Giants.

Q. What Atlanta businessman won nine matches to take the 1938 British Amateur tournament at Troon, Scotland?

A. Charlie Yates.

◆

Q. What Atlanta-born athlete was the only U.S. female to win a gold medal at the 1956 Melbourne Olympics?

A. Mildred McDaniel Singleton, world high jump record of 5 feet, 9¼ inches.

◆

Q. What Tech Hall of Famer was the best offensive lineman for the Buffalo Bills from 1961 to 1969?

A. William L. ("Billy") Shaw.

◆

Q. What two international yachting championships have been won by Ted Turner?

A. Scandinavian Gold Cup and the World Ocean Racing Championship in 1972.

◆

Q. What Marietta High School graduate became known as the dean of American golf writers?

A. Oscar Bane ("Pop") Keeler.

◆

Q. What all-around athlete was the first Georgia interior lineman to play pro for the Philadelphia Eagles in 1933?

A. L. Milton ("Red") Leathers, Jr.

◆

Q. What Lincolnton-born ball player became a 1959 vice president of the Washington Senators?

A. Joseph Walton Haynes.

Q. What Atlanta golfer received the International Championship Golf record by winning fifteen consecutive holes?

A. Watts Gunn.

◆

Q. What winning Georgia college basketball coach retired in 1980?

A. James Boyd Scearce, Georgia Southern College, 501 victories, 284 defeats.

◆

Q. Nicholson native Claude Thomas Tolbert, who retired in 1940 after twenty winning coaching seasons at Atlanta Tech High, was known by what nickname?

A. Gabe.

◆

Q. What Atlanta-area coach developed championship teams and produced star athletes Marty Marion, Buster Mott, and Franklin Brooks?

A. Henry L. ("Hank") Langston.

◆

Q. Valdosta resident William L. Goodloe, Jr., a football player, recruiter, and golfer, was known by what nickname?

A. Dynamite.

◆

Q. What Georgia Peach was known as the Empress of Golf during the 1920s?

A. Alexa Stirling Fraser.

◆

Q. Having attended school at Georgia, Vanderbilt, and Young Harris, what man coached fifty-two years at Gainesville High and Georgia Tech and was known as "the man who never had an enemy"?

A. Joe Pittard.

SCIENCE & NATURE

CHAPTER SIX

Q. What manufacturing machine was invented in 1844 by Dr. John Gorrie of Columbus?

A. Ice machine.

◆

Q. What is the official state insect?

A. Honeybee.

◆

Q. What community is nationally known for its sweet onions?

A. Vidalia.

◆

Q. What name is given to the coastal building material made of oyster shells, lime, and sand?

A. Tabby.

◆

Q. In what city is Patterson Planetarium?

A. Columbus.

Q. What Old World species of large white bird may be seen in the pastures of coastal and southern Georgia?

A. Cattle egret, *Bubulcus ibis*.

———◆———

Q. After continued plantings of cotton, acres of farmland are rendered useless due to the absence of what soil nutrient?

A. Nitrogen.

———◆———

Q. Where in Roswell is the wild animal rehabilitation program?

A. The Chattahoochee Nature Center.

———◆———

Q. About how many small ponds have been created in Georgia largely by the federal Soil Conservation Service?

A. 70,000.

———◆———

Q. What is the largest power company lake in the state?

A. Lake Oconee.

———◆———

Q. What is the estimated age of Lover's Oak in Brunswick?

A. Over 900 years.

———◆———

Q. What Turner County community was founded in 1877 and named for a large tree that came from the yard of Captain James Jackson Henderson?

A. Sycamore.

Q. Which newspaper was first printed on newsprint made from white slash pine?

A. The *Soperton News,* March 31, 1933.

———◆———

Q. What nut-producing tree was introduced to the state in 1905?

A. Papershell pecan.

———◆———

Q. What Savannah industrialist set two around-the-world speed records, in both directions, in the Gulfstream corporate jet?

A. Allen E. Paulsen.

———◆———

Q. What Terrell County town is known as the "World's Largest Spanish Peanut Market"?

A. Dawson.

———◆———

Q. What is the state flower?

A. Cherokee rose.

———◆———

Q. The eastern part of White County is noted for what fire-resistant mineral?

A. Asbestos.

———◆———

Q. What is the deepest lake in the state?

A. Carter Lake, 400 feet.

Q. What is the state's largest fresh-water turtle, weighing up to 150 pounds?

A. Alligator snapper.

───────◆───────

Q. What cotton industry process did Launcelot Johnston discover in 1830?

A. Making cottonseed oil.

───────◆───────

Q. What is the name of the DeKalb County twenty-acre natural wildlife refuge and petting zoo?

A. The Wild Life Trails at Stone Mountain.

───────◆───────

Q. What is the local name for the wild hog of the swamp country?

A. Piney woods rooster.

───────◆───────

Q. What was the chief building material used in the capitol in Atlanta?

A. Indiana oolitic limestone.

───────◆───────

Q. What is the official state fossil?

A. Shark tooth.

───────◆───────

Q. Georgia produces approximately one-half of what national mineral?

A. Manganese ore.

Q. What geological feature, believed to be an ancient coastal sandbar, runs about forty miles north and south along the eastern side of Okefenokee Swamp?

A. Trail Ridge.

———◆———

Q. What is the area of Okefenokee Swamp in square miles?

A. 681.

———◆———

Q. Why did President Franklin D. Roosevelt choose to visit Warm Springs?

A. He believed the buoyant warm water would help his paralysis.

———◆———

Q. Where was the first school of forestry established?

A. University of Georgia, 1906.

———◆———

Q. Shell Bluff, on the Savannah River in Burke County, is noted for what type of fossils?

A. Oyster shells.

———◆———

Q. What four types of poisonous snakes are found in Georgia?

A. Rattlesnake, copperhead, water moccasin, and coral snake.

———◆———

Q. What is the name of the Tifton living history village featuring agricultural displays of rural life before 1900?

A. Agrirama.

Q. Where are the headquarters and gardens of the American Camellia Society?

A. Marshallville.

———◆———

Q. What wild orchid blooms in the Okefenokee Swamp?

A. Rose pogonia.

———◆———

Q. Because of its defense mechanism of playing dead, what is the southern Georgia name given for the spreading or puffing adder?

A. 'Possum.

———◆———

Q. What two nicknames, referring to food products, are given to the state?

A. The Peach State and the Goober State.

———◆———

Q. What is Georgia's chief source of income?

A. Textile mills.

———◆———

Q. Which is the highest earth-filled dam east of the Mississippi?

A. Carters Dam.

———◆———

Q. In 1823 natural history researcher Samuel L. Mitchill began the scientific documentation of fossils by studying what creature found on Skidaway Island?

A. A giant ground sloth.

Q. The Crawford W. Long Medical Museum at Jefferson documents what medical discovery and advancement?

A. Anesthetics, in 1842.

Q. What is Georgia's position among the states as to number of soil types?

A. First, having more than any other.

Q. Georgia is known for what three commercial varieties of peaches?

A. Georgia Bell, Elberta, and Hale.

Q. What wood-finishing oil, made from the nuts of trees, was introduced into the state in 1908?

A. Tung oil.

Q. What area of the state is noted for growing sugar cane?

A. The vicinity of Cairo.

Q. What large red-billed, red-faced wading bird is common along Georgia's coastal region?

A. The white ibis, *Eudocimus albus*.

Q. What area near Blairsville displays Indian stone carvings of bird, animal, and human tracks?

A. Track Rock Archeological Area.

Q. What was the name of the first formal zoo school established in 1960?

A. Atlanta Zoological Gardens.

———◆———

Q. What crop was grown commercially after the boll weevil's attack on cotton production?

A. Peanuts.

———◆———

Q. By the 1930s, twenty-two million acres of Georgia land suffered from what problem?

A. Chronic topsoil erosion.

———◆———

Q. Which state park is named for a tree parasite?

A. Mistletoe State Park.

———◆———

Q. What endangered species of woodpecker may be seen in the Okefenokee Swamp?

A. Red-cockaded woodpecker.

———◆———

Q. How long is the Chattooga River?

A. Fifty miles.

———◆———

Q. What are the two national forests in the state?

A. Chattahoochee and Oconee.

Q. What museum is noted for its rare amethyst collection?

A. Weinman Mineral Center, near Cartersville.

———◆———

Q. Which Stephens County town is named for the Celtic word meaning "island of apples"?

A. Avalon.

———◆———

Q. What is the highest body of water in the state?

A. Conasauga Lake, Murray County, 3,200 feet above sea level.

———◆———

Q. Why is the Coastal Area Research Station in Chatham County called the Bamboo Farm?

A. It ships bamboo to zoos all over the United States for panda food.

———◆———

Q. What river did the Spanish name San Pedro?

A. Suwannee River.

———◆———

Q. Where was the first medical college chartered in 1828?

A. Augusta.

———◆———

Q. What did the Indians call the Okefenokee Swamp?

A. Land of Trembling Earth.

Q. What is the name of the famous gorilla at the Atlanta Zoo?

A. Willie B.

———◆———

Q. What natural resource was harnessed to make Columbus a major manufacturing center?

A. Chattahoochee River.

———◆———

Q. What waterfalls, at 186 feet in height, are higher than Niagara Falls?

A. Toccoa Falls.

———◆———

Q. Development of what process caused peaches to become a major commercial crop after 1890?

A. Refrigeration.

———◆———

Q. What is the state tree?

A. Live oak.

———◆———

Q. In 1918, what Georgian originated the Flanders Field Memorial Poppy as the memorial flower of World War I?

A. Moina Bell Michael.

———◆———

Q. What plant forms the swamp country peat bogs?

A. Sphagnum moss.

SCIENCE & NATURE

Q. Where can the original Apollo 6 space capsule be seen?

A. Fernbank Science Center, Atlanta.

Q. Who is credited with developing the process of making newsprint from pine?

A. Dr. Charles Herty, 1932.

Q. What is the state bird?

A. Brown thrasher.

Q. What city hosts the Fall Leaf Festival?

A. Cleveland.

Q. In the 1930s the area around Griffin became prominent for producing what crop?

A. Pimientos.

Q. What is the name of the wildlife preserve in Albany that provides elevated walkways for the viewing of animals in their natural habitat?

A. Chehaw Wild Animal Park.

Q. What is the largest natural spring in the state?

A. Radium Springs in Dougherty County.

Q. What is another name for the Little Grand Canyon, west of Lumpkin, in Stewart County?

A. Providence Canyon.

———◆———

Q. In what year was the "big fire" in the Okefenokee Swamp?

A. 1844.

———◆———

Q. What Atlanta pharmacist invented Coca-Cola?

A. John Pemberton.

———◆———

Q. How many acres of stacked lumber is maintained on inventory at the Del-Cook Lumber Company of Cook County, the largest lumber company in the eastern United States?

A. Eighty.

———◆———

Q. What unusual geological formation is found in the area of Albany?

A. Fossil sand dunes.

———◆———

Q. What city has one of the twenty-five national test gardens for All-American Roses?

A. Thomasville.

———◆———

Q. What is the largest reptile found in the state?

A. Alligator.

Q. What Marshallville man originated the Elberta peach in 1870?

A. Samuel B. Rumph.

———◆———

Q. What is the enrollment of Georgia Tech, whose College of Engineering is the largest engineering school in the South?

A. 12,500 (in 1994).

———◆———

Q. What flower is believed to grow only within a fifty-mile radius of Stone Mountain?

A. Confederate yellow daisy.

———◆———

Q. What is the largest national wildlife refuge in the eastern United States?

A. Okefenokee National Wildlife Refuge.

———◆———

Q. What two rivers originate in the Okefenokee Swamp?

A. St. Marys and Suwannee.

———◆———

Q. What mineral is refined from Georgia's production of bauxite?

A. Aluminum.

———◆———

Q. In 1842, what method for painless surgery was introduced in Jefferson by Dr. Crawford W. Long?

A. The use of ether as an anesthetic.

Q. What lake is formed by the Chattahoochee and Flint rivers at the Jim Woodruff Dam?

A. Lake Seminole.

———————◆———————

Q. What variety of cotton was introduced from the Bahama Islands in 1786?

A. Sea-island cotton.

———————◆———————

Q. What is the name of the 146-acre retail and wholesale outlet for Georgia farmers?

A. Atlanta State Farmers Market.

———————◆———————

Q. How many species of tropical butterflies inhabit the 4.5-acre Cecil B. Day Butterfly Center at Callaway Gardens?

A. Fifty.

———————◆———————

Q. What famous building in Washington, D.C., is built of Georgian marble?

A. The Lincoln Memorial.

———————◆———————

Q. In what year was the Okefenokee Swamp declared a wildlife refuge?

A. 1937.

———————◆———————

Q. What agricultural region is centered in Ashburn?

A. The peanut belt.

Q. Where are marine exhibits and a "petting" aquarium located?

A. Coastal exhibit room, Georgia Department of Natural Resources, Brunswick.

———◆———

Q. How many state parks are in Georgia?

A. Forty-three.

———◆———

Q. What is the acreage of Stone Mountain?

A. 583.

———◆———

Q. What common trait is shared by the sundew, yellow butterwort, pitcher, and bladderwort plants of the moist, swampy areas?

A. They are insect eaters.

———◆———

Q. What mineral was mined in colonial days from deposits near Augusta and Macon for use at the Wedgewood Pottery in England?

A. Kaolin, a high-grade clay.

———◆———

Q. What major archeological site near Macon houses six different native American cultures from 10,000 B.C. to A.D. 1825?

A. Ocmulgee National Monument.

———◆———

Q. What is the state's highest recorded temperature?

A. 112 degrees F (44 degrees C), Louisville, July 24, 1952.

Q. What lake built by the U.S. Corps of Engineers holds the national record for annual visits?

A. Lake Lanier.

———◆———

Q. What is the popular name for the official state mineral, staurolite?

A. Fairy crosses or fairy stones.

———◆———

Q. What was the first large cash crop to be planted in the Sea Islands?

A. Indigo.

———◆———

Q. What is Georgia's official state fish?

A. Largemouth bass.

———◆———

Q. Where can you find a research center and museum for communications and military signal history?

A. Signal Corps Museum, Fort Gordon.

———◆———

Q. In 1974, the Chattooga River was placed under what federal protection plan?

A. The Wild and Scenic Rivers Act.

———◆———

Q. Stone Mountain granite was used for what Caribbean university building?

A. The University of Havana.

Q. What member of the hare family is noted for its swimming ability in the swamp country?

A. Marsh rabbit.

———◆———

Q. What city hosts the Putnam County Dairy Festival?

A. Eatonton.

———◆———

Q. In what Savannah area may indigenous animals be seen in their natural habitat?

A. Oatland Island.

———◆———

Q. What grayish stemmed, rootless plant can be seen hanging from trees and power lines across the southern portion of the state?

A. Spanish moss, *Tillandsia usneoides*.

———◆———

Q. What does the Latin word *georgicus* mean?

A. Agricultural.

———◆———

Q. Where can one of the largest reptile collections in America be viewed?

A. Atlanta Zoo, Grant Park.

———◆———

Q. What Lincoln County mathematician and engineer predicted the total eclipse of the sun on May 28, 1900, fifty years before it happened?

A. Thomas P. Ashmore (1812–1884).

Q. What Texas bird may be found in some concentration in southeastern coastal Georgia?

A. Plain chachalaca, *Ortalis vetula*.

———◆———

Q. Under what circumstance was ether first used as an anesthetic?

A. Dr. Crawford W. Long administered it to remove a cyst from the neck of James Venable.

———◆———

Q. The interconnecting tidal rivers and creeks of the inland portion of Jekyll and St. Simons islands are known by what name?

A. Marshes of Glynn.

———◆———

Q. What is the state's most valuable farm product?

A. Broiler chickens.

———◆———

Q. By 1763, what river was the western boundary of Georgia?

A. Mississippi River.

———◆———

Q. Which state park is known as the Grand Canyon of North Georgia?

A. Cloudland Canyon State Park.

———◆———

Q. What city hosts the Georgia Marble Festival?

A. Jasper.

Q. What 1848 communications hook-up installed from Augusta to Columbus linked Washington, D.C., with New Orleans?

A. The state's first telegraph.

———◆———

Q. What is Georgia's official state wildflower?

A. Azalea.

———◆———

Q. What is the daily water output of Blue Springs, at the foot of Pine Mountain in Harris County?

A. One million gallons.

———◆———

Q. What county had the first tannery?

A. Lincoln County.

———◆———

Q. What city produces more granite monuments than any other city in the world?

A. Elberton.

———◆———

Q. What gave Blue Bluff in Burke County its name?

A. Blue-gray glauconitic clay.

———◆———

Q. What city is known as the Camellia City of the South?

A. Thomson.

Q. What Georgia site provided the granite that was used in part of the Panama Canal construction?

A. Stone Mountain.

———◆———

Q. What scenic creek in the Chattahoochee National Forest drops 600 feet in less than one mile?

A. Frogtown Creek.

———◆———

Q. What is the official state gem, named in 1976?

A. Quartz.

———◆———

Q. What is the official state game bird, named in 1970?

A. Bobwhite quail.

———◆———

Q. Georgia ranks second in the national production of what building stone?

A. Marble.

———◆———

Q. What river has its upper limit in Gilmer County, flowing 729 miles later into the Mobile River?

A. Alabama.

———◆———

Q. Where may special nature trails for heart patients and the visually impaired be found?

A. Fernbank Science Center, Atlanta.

Q. Where is the University of Georgia Marine Institute?

A. Sapelo Island.

◆

Q. What is the acreage of the bald on Brasstown Bald?

A. Three-fourths of an acre.

◆

Q. What nutrient-rich plant, producing up to ten tons to the acre, is important to the ecological food chain of the coastal region?

A. Marsh grass.

◆

Q. In what year did a tornado tear through Mississippi into Gainesville, taking a total of 658 lives?

A. 1936.

◆

Q. What insect first attacked the cottonfields in 1921?

A. Boll weevil.

◆

Q. Georgia is the national leader in the production of what porous, claylike material used in various industrial processes?

A. Fuller's earth.

◆

Q. Where is the geographic center of Georgia?

A. Twiggs County, eighteen miles southeast of Macon.

◆

Q. Forests cover approximately what percentage of Georgia?

A. 70 percent.

Q. What is Georgia's most valuable cash crop?

A. Peanuts.

◆

Q. What is the local name for the dense swamp area in upper Laurens County?

A. Cow Hell.

◆

Q. What internationally known naturalist and wildlife expert designed the Black Rhinoceros exhibit at the Atlanta Zoo?

A. Jim Fowler.

◆

Q. Who was Georgia's first woman doctor?

A. Dr. Loree Florence of Lincoln County.

◆

Q. A giant 300-foot-diameter mound on Sapelo Island, typifying Georgia's first Indian mounds, is composed of what material?

A. Saltwater shells.

◆

Q. The Museum of Arts and Sciences and the Mark Smith Planetarium are in which city?

A. Macon.

◆

Q. How many lives were lost in a train wreck that occurred near Stockton on August 4, 1944?

A. Forty-seven.

Q. The grounds of Callanwolde Fine Arts Center in Atlanta, the former home of Charles Howard Candler, past-president of Coca-Cola, were designed by what famous landscape artist?

A. Frederick Law Olmstead, designer of New York City's Central Park.

------◆------

Q. What is the function of the cotton gin?

A. It removes cotton fibers from the cotton seed.

------◆------

Q. What famous battleship was constructed from the live oaks on Gascoigne Bluff?

A. The *Constitution* ("Old Ironsides").

------◆------

Q. What river separates Little St. Simons Island from St. Simons Island?

A. Hampton River.

------◆------

Q. What museum, opened in 1981, displays exhibits, artifacts, and educational information about one of northeast Georgia's largest industries?

A. Elberton Granite Museum and Exhibit.

------◆------

Q. Who was the first physician of Stewart County?

A. Dr. Bryan Bedingfield.

------◆------

Q. What type of federal project, featuring twenty-six large tank aquariums, is located near Millen?

A. National Fish Hatchery.

Q. What tree, common in the southern swamps and noted for its "knees," may reach a height of 120 feet?

A. Cypress.

———————◆———————

Q. The first bauxite discovery in the United States in 1887 was made near what northwestern community?

A. Rome.

———————◆———————

Q. What Georgia city calls itself the Quail Hunting Capital of the World?

A. Albany.

———————◆———————

Q. What ethnic group was extensively researched in the 1890s by James Mooney for the Smithsonian Institution's Bureau of American Ethnology?

A. Cherokee Indians.

———————◆———————

Q. What is the acreage of the Okefenokee Swamp?

A. 438,000 acres.

———————◆———————

Q. What lizard is the swiftest and most elusive in the state?

A. The six-lined race runner or race nag.

———————◆———————

Q. What is Georgia's national rank in pecan production?

A. First.

Q. What is the second-ranking cash crop in Georgia?

A. Soybeans.

———◆———

Q. Where is the state's largest apple-growing center?

A. Cornelia.

———◆———

Q. What is the common name for the large marshes in Okefenokee Swamp?

A. Prairies.

———◆———

Q. What is the geological feature created by the division between the Piedmont Plateau and the Coastal Plain?

A. The Fall Line.

———◆———

Q. Georgia is the second national producer of what soft, heavy, silver-colored metallic element?

A. Barite, from which barium is processed.

———◆———

Q. What type of trees was planted by colonists to help establish a silk industry in Georgia?

A. Mulberry.

———◆———

Q. What national military park is the oldest, largest, and most visited?

A. Chickamauga National Military Park.

Q. What is the real name of the Georgia "Goat Man," who drove a cart pulled by goats between Macon and Monteagle, Tennessee, in the 1940s, 1950s, and 1960s?

A. Chesney McCartney.

———◆———

Q. What brightly colored, red, blue and yellow-green bird may be seen along the coastal regions in the summer?

A. Painted bunting, *Passerina ciris*.

———◆———

Q. What type of flower, in over 400 varieties, is shipped throughout the world from Perry?

A. Day lilies.

———◆———

Q. Where was Georgia's first paper mill located?

A. Scull Shoals.

———◆———

Q. What name does tradition say was given to the Suwannee River by the Maya Indians from the Yucatan?

A. Water Beloved of the Sun God.

———◆———

Q. What annual Atlanta event benefits the Henrietta Egleston Hospital for critically ill children?

A. The Festival of Trees, December.

———◆———

Q. What Quaker naturalist and trailblazer visited Georgia in 1765 and 1773?

A. William Bartram.

Q. What official designation was given Cumberland Island in 1972?

A. National Seashore.

Q. Which historic site was once owned by Tiffany's of New York?

A. Graves Mountain, southwest of Lincolnton.

Q. Where is a thirty-eight-foot model of a loblolly pine to be found?

A. Southern Forest World, Waycross.

Q. What is the annual apple harvest in Gilmer County?

A. 200,000 bushels.

Q. What Dalton company had its former offices in the Crown Gardens and Archives?

A. Crown Cotton Mills.

Q. What rare species of small tree was discovered growing naturally only in Georgia by John and William Bartram in 1765?

A. Lost camelia, *Franklinia* or *Gordonia altamaha*.

Q. What is the actual name of the color-changing lizard known as the American chameleon?

A. The green anole.

Q. What is the name of the world's smallest fish that is found in the Okefenokee Swamp?

A. Pygmy killifish.

———◆———

Q. What is the collective name of the 153-foot waterfall on Curtis Creek and the 50-foot waterfall on York Creek?

A. Anna Ruby Falls.

———◆———

Q. Which state park is located in Cobb and Fulton counties?

A. Chattahoochee Palisades State Park.

———◆———

Q. What was the production level of corn in the state at the outbreak of the Civil War in 1861?

A. Thirty million bushels.

———◆———

Q. What is Athens's most unusual property owner, at Dearing and Finley streets?

A. An oak, the Tree That Owns Itself, deeded possession of its land by a former owner grateful for its shade.

———◆———

Q. Trees of foreign origin, including the tung and Chinese pistachio, surround the courthouse of which city?

A. Brunswick.

———◆———

Q. What coastal museum illustrates the rice and dairy farms of the last century?

A. Hofwyl-Broadfield Plantation near Brunswick.

Q. The southern Indians enjoyed the black fruit of what common American palm?

A. Saw palmetto.

———◆———

Q. What is the name of the world's most advanced green-house complex featured at Callaway Gardens?

A. John A. Sibley Horticultural Center.

———◆———

Q. What is the Creek Indian translation of Lochochee Creek in Terrell County?

A. "Little Turtle."

———◆———

Q. McCranier's Turpentine Still is near what community?

A. Willacoochee.

———◆———

Q. What Georgian legless lizard is often mistaken for a snake?

A. Glass lizard.

———◆———

Q. How many ingredients are found in Coca-Cola?

A. Fifteen.

———◆———

Q. What is the lowest recorded temperature on Brasstown Bald?

A. −27 degrees F.